So Much to Live For

A Memoir
of Love, Loss and Living On

Jennifer Hamlin Church

To Peggy ~
With affection ~
To a Saint!
Jennifer

ISBN 978-1-312-04705-1

Published in 2014 by Jennifer Hamlin Church
Printed in the United States of America

Cover design by John MacNaughton.
Cover photography by Jennifer Hamlin Church.
Book design by John MacNaughton and Jennifer Church.

An earlier version of "A Wink and A Smile"
appeared in the 2013 edition of *Eclipse*
published by Siena Heights University.

"A Valediction" is reprinted by permission
of the poet, Patricia Schnapp, RSM.

For My Girls:

Cindy, Sarah and Michelle

Even on a cold gray morning
  We can see the sunlight shine.

Bill Staines, "All of Me"

Love. Love changes everything:
  How we live and how we die.

Don Black and Charles Hart,
"Love Changes Everything"

So Much to Live For

Contents

Last Words

"Don't be surprised if I hug you to death."

This were my husband's last spoken words to me. It was the summer of 2004. We were speaking by telephone, he with difficulty from a hospital bed at the Ohio State University Medical Center in Columbus, I from my desk in the advancement office at Siena Heights University, 165 miles away in Adrian, Michigan.

He had been taken by ambulance the night before from Toledo Hospital, near our home by the Michigan-Ohio border, to the Surgical Intensive Care Unit at Ohio State where he had received his second kidney transplant just three weeks earlier.

Our older daughters, Cindy and Sarah, had joked that their younger sister, Michelle, trumped them for life with her Father's Day gift of one of her healthy 24-year-old kidneys. The surgery went well for both Michelle and her dad.

Not long after returning home, though, Tracy's recovery seemed to stall, and then go backward. "Failure to thrive" was how I described it, when I first called OSU. But Tracy's "numbers"—the measurements of kidney function assessed by a local lab several times a week—were good, so the OSU transplant staff advised us to keep working with our local doctors. We did. But his condition deteriorated.

When he could no longer get up from the couch, I bought a lift chair. And made more medical appointments. A few days later, the doctors diagnosed pneumonia.

Tracy was admitted to Toledo Hospital.

Pneumonia is a scary diagnosis for anyone in fragile health; for someone with a compromised immune system, it is seriously threatening. Tracy, by now, had had three organ transplants—a kidney in 1989, a pancreas in 1998, and now this replacement kidney in 2004—and he was on a complicated program of immune suppression to enable the multiple "foreign bodies" to do their work inside his body. The nephrologist in Toledo pulled no punches at the end of a long day of evaluation: "He is very sick," he said, after guiding me into the hallway outside Tracy's room.

"This will be a long fight. We can only hope his heart is strong enough for it."

Two days later, the doctors in both Toledo and Columbus agreed he should be in the care of the OSU transplant team; and so, late at night, after hours of hurry-up-and-wait, Tracy was transferred by ambulance 140-plus miles south to the OSU Medical Center.

"You stay," Tracy told me that night. "You need to go to work." I already had taken time off for the kidney transplant. And then there was the matter of my own doctor's appointment the next day. I had delayed it several times already, and I was a relatively new cancer survivor.

"You need to take care of yourself, too," he admonished me.

So, now, here I was, on the phone from work for the third time on Tracy's first day in Columbus. With each call, his voice had been more choked, the effort to speak more difficult as pneumonia gripped his lungs and anxiety gripped his mind. He didn't want to worry me; he never wanted to worry me. But it was time for me to take charge.

"I am coming down right after I see my doctor," I said firmly.

"You...don't...have to," he choked out in a thin and raspy voice.

"But I am going to," I replied, dismissing all argument. "I am coming. I will see you as soon as I can get there."

And then he said it.

"Don't...be surprised...if I hug you...to death."

I did not know then, or for weeks to come, that I would not again hear him say my name, that he would never tell me another joke, or ask my views on the day's headline news, or call to me for help with a shoe or a pill box or a story he was writing. By the time I arrived that night, the effort of breathing would take all the energy he had; and by the next morning, he would have a ventilator tube in his throat to keep him breathing. There would be no talking.

But I did not know any of that when I hung up the phone. All I knew at that moment was that he was sick, he was afraid (I could hear it, and this was unusual), and he loved me. Needed me. Wanted me.

Don't be surprised if I hug you to death.
Last words. What a gift they turned out to be.

Bargaining With God

Shortly before my wedding in 1990, I met with the minister who would be performing the ceremony. She was a friend, the wife of my boss, and we sat together in my office on the second floor of the gracious alumni center at Ohio Wesleyan University in Delaware, Ohio, just north of Columbus.

My husband-to-be, who lived three hours away in Michigan, was to join us. This was, after all, the traditional opportunity for couples counseling that most clergy recommend, if not require, before officiating at a marriage ceremony. We already had rescheduled the meeting several times to accommodate my fiance's unpredictable schedule, so that now the wedding date was less than two weeks away.

But once again, circumstances had changed. Instead of sitting in one of the upholstered guest chairs in my office, Tracy was lying in a hospital bed, nursing a persistent foot wound that refused to heal despite four months of regular care and several prior hospital stays.

The minister was understanding; the three of us would have time for a pastoral visit a day or two before the wedding, when we all gathered in Maine. For today, she would meet just with me, one on one.

She asked about the journey that had brought us to our decision to marry. I described our seven-year friendship: the unexpected meeting through friends, our immediate attraction through words, the instant interest in talking together about anything, everything—religion, education, nature, animals, children, art, language, politics.

I recalled the difficulties and detours, was honest about the obstacles: He was married, a husband already for nearly seventeen years when we met, father of three children. He took his marriage vows—his word of honor—as seriously as was possible; far more seriously, in fact, than most people seemed to in the early 1980s. I was a never-married single woman, public relations director for a United Methodist college; and I believed that, regardless of the free-love mantra that had surrounded my coming of age in the late '60s and early '70s, one simply did not get involved with a married man. Why would anyone risk hurting so many people?

We had traveled a complicated road of twists, turns, tears, separations and reconnections until now, seven years, several moves and a few medical roller coasters later, here we were, days away from flying to Maine for a summer wedding.

But he was not here. He was in the hospital for the third time that spring, fighting with an open sore that didn't want to close up. It had something to do with the immune suppressants he had begun taking in November, when a kidney transplant had ended a year on dialysis. One family's tragedy was our miracle. Just in time for us to close on the purchase of a house, get engaged and plan a wedding, Tracy got a second chance at vigorous good health...and a drug "habit" that would be part of the rest of his life. Immune suppressants—tiny pills, horse tablets and a sticky liquid that smelled like skunk—kept his body from rejecting the kidney (a good thing) and prevented a simple cut on his foot from healing (not good).

"I'm getting married in Maine," he had told the doctors this time. "We've got five days to get this wrapped up."

Mary, the minister, reflected on the ragged road we had travelled from our first chance meeting to our decision to marry. "You've been through a lot to get to where you are," she observed. "What do you see in your future? How do you see your life together? What do you hope for?"

I remember pausing. She was, after all, a minister.

"I know Tracy has health problems," I answered finally, "so I've been bargaining with God.

"I've asked Him for five years," I said. "Just five years. 'Give us five good years and I'll be satisfied.' I'll take that."

Apparently my answer satisfied Mary that I knew what I was getting into: I was a woman in love, but my eyes were wide open to the darker possibilities that life might, or was likely to, throw at us.

And maybe she was right.

For years after we were married, I downplayed the numbers of our wedding anniversaries: not the celebrations—I was always ready to mark those occasions with festivity and another viewing of the homemade wedding video—but the actual numbers. If I ignore the specifics, I reasoned, the twelfth and the eighteenth years will come as naturally as the first and second. But to pay attention to each numbered year, to actually keep count? That would surely jinx Tracy, I felt in some deep and unspoken way. That would jinx us. So we celebrated without giving much thought to the numbers.

In the same way, I never marked the specific anniversary of the kidney transplant.

Five years was the average life span of a transplanted cadaver kidney, we were told in 1989 when Tracy received that precious gift; so I recognized that date only silently, secretly. Tracy, who found it hard even to remember birthdays, rarely mentioned it; and to the rest of the family, the medical landmark passed by blissfully unnoticed. That November date came and went each year, unremarked amid the annual Thanksgiving hubbub.

I began to relax when we reached year seven of life with each other, and with someone else's kidney. Six months later, we were confident enough to pursue the possibility of a second transplant, a pancreas this time that would end Tracy's dependence on insulin shots—though it would not, we discovered, change his status as a diabetic. Regardless of miraculous medical interventions, he would always be classified within the health profession as a Type I (juvenile onset) diabetic. Now the daily drugs kept in check his body's war on two foreign systems.

The year that followed the pancreas transplant was a hard one. "Do you think I asked for too much?" Tracy queried weakly, sitting in the early summer sunshine on our back porch, in his dark green bathrobe, about two weeks after that surgery. He, too, had been bargaining with God. Maybe he had pushed his luck too far?

"No," I replied. "We just have to work out the kinks." I was chipper, staunch, more confident outwardly than I felt inside but firm in my resolve to keep his spirits up, keep him going. "We'll get it worked out."

Eleven months, five hospitalizations and one major surgery later, it got worked out.

By then, we were long past the five years of togetherness I had asked for. The bargain was...not forgotten, never forgotten...but filed away, far back in the bottom drawer of my mind. Life was ours to live. And to love. And we did, embracing the lows as well as the highs, the stormy days as well as the sweet sunny mornings.

Through it all, we both worked, as we always had. Tracy continued as vice president and general manager of a small manufacturing firm, combining his mechanical creativity and competitive nature in the development of transmission testing machines. He traveled a lot, both in the U.S. and overseas, marketing these room-sized machines. I continued as public relations director at Ohio Wesleyan, spending several days a week in central Ohio, then working at home in Michigan via computer, fax and telephone. I co-chaired the university's year-long 150th anniversary celebration and coordinated the inauguration of a new university president.

Then, we both lost our jobs. Tracy arrived one day to find the lock on his office door changed and a box for him to fill with his personal things; the owner's son-in-law was taking over. I got two months' notice when the new president decided to balance the budget by eliminating a dean and two directors, dividing our responsibilities up among our staffs.

Thankfully, we did not lose our jobs at the same time, and we both survived that blow to economic and psychological security. Tracy fulfilled a lifelong dream by starting his own company, designing and building hydraulic equipment for clients ranging from international automakers to small environmental firms. After a month on unemployment, I took over communications and alumni relations at Siena Heights University, immediately discovering the joys of living and working in the same state and coming home to Tracy every night. Our combined income dropped by two-thirds, but we managed. We stopped going out for dinner so often, amazed at how much we'd been spending on mediocre meals, and began to enjoy cooking together.

As the years went by, we shared the joys and fears and confusions presented by our growing young-adult children. I learned how to cheer at middle-school, then high-school, basketball and volleyball games. We learned to pick our battles with the girls, choosing when to take the bait and when to ignore the abrasive rap music, or questionable fashion choice, or whatever else might seem to us inappropriate. Like all parents, we agonized over our girls' decisions and dilemmas: the academic achievements and disasters, job successes and failures, romantic mishaps and marriage choices.

When we reached our tenth anniversary, and the first two grandchildren were 13 and 8, Cindy became pregnant a third time, then Sarah and Michelle followed suit. Four grandchildren arrived in two years. Never having had babies of my own, I delighted in these little ones who brought no baggage to our relationship, welcoming me without reservation as Grandma Jennifer.

And always, in the midst of everything, we handled whatever medical speed bumps and dead ends waited for Tracy in the road ahead: foot problems, heart irregularities, circulation disorders, nerve deterioration, and any cold or flu bug that found its way into Tracy's system. The immune suppressants that kept his kidney functioning well past five years, and then his pancreas, too, also turned any wound, virus or bacterium into at least a two-week illness. A simple blister on his foot could put Tracy on crutches for six weeks. For him, there was no such thing as a "minor" infection.

"I don't know how you cope," a friend once said to us.

We reflected wryly on that comment many times. Coping was not such an amazing skill, we concluded; it was really the only choice. You could lie around and mope, be cranky and angry with the world; or you could find something else to do while waiting to do what you really wanted. You managed to survive. Or else you gave up—and who wanted to do that? Not us.

"How do you cope?"

We just did, finding new reasons to laugh, new ways to play, new things to talk about.

"Please, God, give us five years," I had prayed. Pleaded. "Just five years." We got fourteen. It was a good gamble.

But even fourteen years was not enough. I wanted more time. And so did he. Until the very end.

Wild and Free
Growing Up in the '50s

Tracy and I grew up in the 1950s, a decade derided just a few years later as bland, boring, and all-too-predictable: an era of outdated inhibitions and shallow lives.

Television sets entered middle-class homes in the '50s, bringing us Leave It to Beaver, Ozzie and Harriet and Father Knows Best, with their enduring stereotypes of middle-class family life: Mothers wore high heels and pearls, cooking, cleaning and raising children in perfectly pressed domesticity. Fathers went calmly to work in suits, came home with a smile, and sat down to cordial home-made family dinners. No one got in serious trouble, not even the smarmy Eddie Haskell, and everyone was successful and content.

By the late 1960s, Vietnam, civil rights, drugs and the sexual revolution had inalterably changed the picture of real life, and student protesters across the country blamed most of the problems, and the entire "military-industrial complex" that they said produced them, on the previous generation (our mothers and fathers) and the emotional repression of the Eisenhower years.

I know. I remember hearing it all and thinking it might be true. Though not a rabble-rouser, I was idealistic. I protested, too, first watching from a Boston sidewalk in the summer of 1969, then joining thousands of others—students, retirees, artists, housewives and businessmen—in the March on Washington later that fall. I could see that our country had problems and needed change. I didn't know all the causes, but, hey, maybe the "establishment" was to blame. Maybe our parents had it all wrong.

The fifties look different to me now.

I don't believe the Cleavers ever really existed, even when Beaver and his family were cavorting on our grainy black-and-white television screens every week. Family life was never quite that "perfect" or antiseptic. Still, every family I knew in the '50s included two parents (and only one of them worked). Those families all sat down together to eat, at least for dinner; and kids of all ages respected, even expected, playtime interference from other kids' mothers, considering most adults to be somewhat legitimate authority figures.

Was that good? It wasn't terrible; that much I believe. Were there hidden dangers, nasty villains among those authority-figure adults? A few, for sure.

Nonetheless, in those years, two children growing up in very different families and communities, in distinctly different segments of American society, reached the same conclusion: Life was anything but bland, boring and predictable. In fact, life was pretty darned great.

"No one had more freedom than a 12-year-old farm boy in the 1950s," Tracy once said, recalling his childhood in a rural, largely agricultural community in southeast Michigan. Roaming at will through woods, fields and farmsteads, he learned that boyish curiosity and polite respect won the tolerance of most country characters, even the gruffest of hermits.

I felt pretty much the same way.

"I think life is just about perfect right now," I wrote at age 12 from my east coast suburban home, after spending two glorious weeks at sleep-away camp. I may not have used those exact words, but I remember clearly what I thought and felt as I wrote to the now-nameless red-headed counselor who had overseen my cabin at Camp Kiwanee: Boys were good, horses were better, and life stretched ahead sparkling with possibility and adventure.

From first grade through sixth, the standard range for elementary school at the time, I walked three-quarters of a mile to school and back, twice a day including the trip home for lunch. Our neighborhood in a suburb of Boston, Massachusetts, was full of young families with children, all living in two-story houses, one next to the other, each with what we thought at the time was a large front yard and a bigger back yard.

On the first few days of school each year, nervous mothers gathered proudly to walk the first-graders to the end of our road, and watch them cross Commercial Street under the watchful eye of a fifth- or sixth-grader wearing the white sash of the Safety Patrol. Moms would linger, waving the little ones on across Legion Field toward the next intersection, where the jovial white-haired Officer Riley would shepherd them across the other busy street between home and the elementary school, a few blocks past the aging high school.

All year long, we kids walked to school, often in bunches, sometimes by ourselves if we were feeling solitary. The girls wore dresses, with slacks underneath in winter; the boys wore trousers and collared shirts, with pint-size sport coats on picture days. If it was particularly rainy, someone's father might drive us to school on his way to work; or a mom might be waiting in the car after school if the dad had carpooled to work that day. (Except for the family that owned the taxi service, no one we knew had two cars.) And if you dawdled in the morning or after lunch, there was no back-up transportation to whisk you to school. If you were late, you ran.

On days when I walked alone, I stopped at the top of our road to saddle my imaginary horse. Blackie was a handsome stallion from the herd of china horses that lived on a shelf in my bedroom, figurines I had been collecting for as long as I could remember. "Easy, Blackie," I crooned, tightening the girth and slipping on the bridle in mime. "Good boy. Okay, let's go." And Blackie and I would walk, trot and canter through the brilliant colors of a New England fall, down sparkling snowy winter streets, or past the fragrant lilacs of spring. Somewhere along the way, I dismounted, turning him into the "pasture" of some back yard. "You be good, now, Blackie. I'll see you later."

And on I went at a normal walk to Academy Avenue School.

The school held twelve classrooms, two each for six grades. The first floor housed the lower grades and the lunchroom, where those who came by bus bought milk to go with whatever lunchbox fare they brought from home. The upper grades and the auditorium were on the second floor. The school was built into a hill, allowing each floor to open onto its own playground for recess. The 375 or so students in the school were marshaled, managed, guided and disciplined by our classroom teachers, the kindly school custodian (husband of my first grade teacher), and our principal, the fierce and diminutive Miss Reddy.

Miss Reddy was a force to be reckoned with—or, preferably, to be avoided. With her kinky white hair, she seemed as old as the hills but there was nothing weak about her. Miss Reddy ruled the school with a general's iron will, dictating that students walk in single file in the hallway, always "on the white line." (Parallel rows of white tiles traveled down the right and left sides of every hallway, turning the blue linoleum floors into highways through the school.) In Miss Reddy's world, there was no talking in the halls, no talking in the lunch room. Students in the first three grades wrote exclusively with pencil. Beginning in the fourth grade, we wrote in pen—quill pens with replaceable nibs, dipped into the inkwells in the upper right corners of the desks. (Lefties just had to reach.) Possession or use of a ball point pen was grounds for a serious trip to Miss Reddy's office.

Miss Reddy inspired fear in the toughest of students. I saw her crumple the bravado of a heavyset fifth grade boy who towered over her when she stood toe to toe in her lace-up black librarian heels, chin jutting upward into his chest, to dismiss him as a "Bully!" Whatever bullying he had been doing, ceased.

It was a restrictive, disciplined approach. My sister and brother and I all thrived; but no doubt that was partly because we were smart—and because we had sensible parents who nurtured, supported, nudged and encouraged us at home. Some other students, who might have needed more of that in the classroom, probably didn't blossom as well in that environment. And teachers did not always make honorable or sensible choices in their teaching methods. A fourth-grade teacher, stern but beloved, almost embarrassed my incredibly bright older sister into mediocrity by trying to motivate the other students with a "Beat Rebecca!" contest. My own sixth-grade teacher—the first man teacher of my life, exciting to me for that alone—once crossed a line that even I, naive at the age of 12, recognized, resented and could never forgive: "You don't even deserve to wear that Girl Scout uniform you've got on," he shouted at a friend of mine who had talked in class once too often. "You'd look pretty funny if I came over and took it off you right now—wouldn't you?"

In the shocked silence following that remark, you could have heard a pin drop. Or the death knell of my unquestioned respect for teachers.

But we survived those years. Rebecca did not retreat to mediocrity. And my friend, the Girl Scout, went on to become a social worker, crossing paths with my sister many years later. Miss Reddy retired, taking with her the ink wells and dip pens. Miss Wells, the demanding fourth grade teacher, left us with construction-paper notebook projects on Ancient Greece and Rome that would put some high school students to shame today. The sixth grade teacher moved on to become a principal, before running afoul of the law.

It was not a perfect time, but we grew up unafraid of the world around us. By fourth or fifth grade, we were riding miles on our bicycles—just us kids, no grown-ups—to go to the library or the first McDonald's. We spent long Saturdays in the woods with only our imaginations, a paper bag lunch, and a best friend, a "BFF" in today's kid lingo. Summer evenings after dinner, we stayed outdoors until dark, playing "Kick the Can" up and down the street, in and out of every yard, with gangs of kids of all ages.

I debated the existence of Santa Claus with one BFF, as we sat on big rocks in front of her house one mild December Saturday. "I know there's a Santa Claus," she said confidently, "because he brought us a television last year. I know my parents couldn't afford that." Decades later, when we reconnected over dinner in a restaurant, she told me how much she enjoyed having supper at my house in those days. There were six children in her family and dinnertime was a fast and focused affair; if you wanted a second helping, you had to be among the first to ask. "Your family was so different," she recalled. "You ate slowly and everyone talked. And you could still have seconds." Then she asked: "Does your father still kiss your mother every night before he sits down for supper?" I had never really thought about it; but, yes, he did.

Life in our neighborhood was not perfect. There were a few bullies, though the bullying of those days seems rather innocent today; and kids were not always kind. But we negotiated the ups and downs of friendship, dealt with winning and losing, recognized the differences among our families, and learned to make our own choices. And we did it mostly on our own. We spent a lot of time independent and unsupervised—but we knew everyone's mother could discipline us or send us home. And we knew those mothers were there if we needed them.

Half a country and a world away, Tracy was exploring the forests and farmland of southeast Michigan. He and his best friend, who lived a country block apart, sometimes communicated at night by blinking the lights in their upstairs bedrooms. Weekends and after school, they traipsed the hills and woods for several miles in all directions. They built birdhouses and go-karts and a bridge across the creek in the woods. They listened and learned as their fathers shared the casual wisdom of hunter, gatherer, farmer and mechanic.

When Tracy was 10, his dad began teaching him to shoot. Tracy lay on his stomach on the front lawn, aiming his new pellet gun toward the hill that rose beside and behind the farmhouse. Next to him, sitting back on his heels, his father explained the proper use of the gun, how to hold the stock against his cheek and set up a proper sight line down the barrel, and later, how to disassemble, clean and care for the weapon. How to respect the gun and its power; how to use it honorably and safely.

By the time he was 12, Tracy and his pal usually grabbed their guns before heading outdoors after school. They shot at squirrels, rabbits, birds. When they hit the mark, they stopped to study their prey: How did this wing move? What had this bird eaten? Would you always find this creature near this kind of berry? They learned to open, skin, filet and cook their quarry. When they were older, they earned summer spending money by shooting marauding blackbirds for hire at a nearby orchard, pennies per bird.

They went long distances by bicycle, pedaling down country roads to reach other farms, other adventures. Summer nights, they sneaked up the hill behind the drive-in for silent views of grown-up kisses and more. Oblivious to fire safety, they hid in a neighbor's hayloft and learned to smoke; it was a habit Tracy would steel himself to unlearn years later when it became a matter of life and limb, rather than excitement and boredom.

When the call of the wild mixed with an interest in money, Tracy started a winter trap line, rising in the dark before school to walk the area creeks, checking his lethal traps for muskrats, and walking the line again in the dark of evening. He sent his pelts to faraway furriers; letters from New York City brought back payment.

Most of the kids at the new Madison Agricultural School came from similar families. Madison was its own school district, a rural neighborhood that extended for miles, with big open spaces separating one homestead from another. Everyone from kindergarten through high school attended school in the same building; and until they were old enough to drive whatever wheels they could get their hands on, they all rode the bus. Tracy's bus driver in the early years, Miss Gorney, was also his kindergarten teacher, his minister and, later, his advisor for the Boy Scout God and Country merit program. When 9-year-old Tracy wrote a bad word in the steamed-up back window of the school bus, carefully lettering it backward so it could be read by those outside, it was Miss Gorney—with a clear view in her rear-view mirror of the offense and the nicely reversed word—who handled the discipline and the conversation with Tracy's mother. Ears were boxed at home, and sometimes at school, too. Farm boys were known to fight each other outside; and teachers occasionally put a misbehaving boy up against a locker in the hallways. Thirty or more desks filled each elementary classroom at Madison; Tracy's black-and-white class pictures, like my own, show as many as thirty-four kids lined up, girls sitting on benches in the front, boys standing tall in the back, and a single teacher smiling from the side.

Even as a little boy, Tracy had shown an interest in the world around him. His mother, Florence, walked the fields with him when he was a preschooler, sharing all she knew about trees and wild flowers; she read stories and poems to him at home, where he was her only daytime company at their lonely farm in the country. Once he could read by himself, he never missed a visit with the bookmobile, which became a highlight of summer days. From his father, Vohne, a tool and die maker and part-time farmer, he gained an early interest in how some things grow and others are built. Soon, he was working on engines, itching to move from a backyard go-kart to a souped-up Chevy and a speedy motorcycle. Before long, he was ready to race with the world, or anyone who had the wheels.

By the 1960s, Tracy's teachers called him smart. And sometimes they called him trouble.

By the time Tracy and I met in the early 1980s, I was 32 and he was 34. But we both had strong connections to our family homes and we loved sharing the stories of our 1950s childhoods. From those very different experiences, we both entered our teens with curiosity, a love of the outdoors and a well-established reading habit. We had big dreams and a spirit of adventure.

Changes
Coming of Age in the '60s

The times were changing. Bob Dylan knew it. So did Martin Luther King, Jr. and Malcolm X. And Janice Joplin and Janis Ian. And the non-violent members of the Student Nonviolent Coordinating Committee and the sometimes violent members of Students for a Democratic Society. From John F. Kennedy's election in 1960, to his assassination three years later, to the killings of King and Robert F. Kennedy just two months apart in 1968; from the Cuban missile crisis to the My Lai massacre; from the Beatles to psychedic rock, the 1967 Summer of Love, and 1969's Woodstock and moon walk (the real thing): there was little about American life that did not change during the tumultuous 1960s.

We grew up in the midst of all that. And yet, Tracy and I, each in our own little piece of America, were not even vaguely aware that major shifts might be occurring in society. It all seemed, to us, just the way it was. We were kids, after all, and then teenagers. We heard about civil rights and Vietnam and drugs and the women's movement, but for the most part, our lives were dominated by the more personally vital issues of high school drama, young love and teenage social angst. In that, we were no different from other generations. My mother wondered for a long time why she could not remember being aware of D-Day; years later, she realized that she had graduated from high school on June 7, 1944, and her primary concern at the time was the diminishing pool of potential summer boyfriends in her northern Minnesota mining town.

Despite our casual disregard for the more important social changes going on around us, Tracy in the Midwest and I in New England both experienced the 1960s as a time of significant change. But it was change on an individual level. For him, it was disease that altered the personal landscape: a diagnosis that would shape the rest of his life. For me, it was an entirely new landscape that reshaped my world: a family move from small-town Massachusetts to the suburbs of New York City.

In December 1961, a week before Christmas, Tracy was admitted to Bixby Hospital in Adrian, Michigan. He was 13, half way through eighth grade; and he had just been diagnosed with juvenile diabetes. Except for a few hours at home on Christmas Day, he remained in the hospital for two weeks, finally released on New Year's Eve, Sunday, December 31.

At a school Christmas program, Tracy's best friend's mother mentioned to Florence that Tracy had gotten awfully thin. Florence at first was annoyed by the remark; why was another mother commenting on her child? Later, she was mortified.

"I should have noticed," she confessed to me many years later. "But he was a teenage boy. I never saw him without clothes." Larrie's mother *had* noticed, perhaps when the boys were wrestling or engaged in some kind of wild horseplay.

At home after the Christmas program, Florence told Tracy to lift his shirt. She was shocked. Tracy ate as much as he ever had, and drank milk voraciously, enough to have engendered his father's anger on at least one occasion: "Nothing more to drink until you finish your supper!" But inside his clothes, he was shrinking.

Florence by then had been working at a pharmacy for a few years and she had a better-than-average awareness of health hazards and disease. She was worried. After a few tests, the doctor confirmed her deepest fear: Tracy was diabetic. He was admitted to Bixby immediately.

Diabetes mellitus was observed as much as 2,500 years ago, documented by writers in ancient Egypt and Greece. The word diabetes comes from the Greek for "siphon" in reference to frequent urination; mellitus comes from the Latin for "honey" referring to the excess sugar found in the blood and urine of diabetic patients. For centuries, doctors recognized this wasting disease by its deadly combination of symptoms—excessive thirst and urination, high sugar levels, unstoppable weight loss—but were mystified by the cause. By the early 20th century, researchers had determined that diabetics, who were almost always children, could not metabolize the nutrition in the food they ate. Early photos show young patients in increasingly skeletal condition. The treatment, in those early years, was almost as bad as the disease; doctors advised diets so limited as to verge on starvation. Even so, death was the inevitable outcome.

Tracy's diagnosis in December 1961 came just forty years after the first successful efforts to counteract the disease. In January 1922, British researchers reported cautiously, "We have obtained from the pancreas of animals a mysterious something which when injected into totally diabetic dogs completely removes all the cardinal symptoms of the disease. If the substance works on the human, it will be a great boon to medicine."

Indeed, insulin—the "mysterious something"—would prove to be a lifesaving benefit and a great advance to medicine; but medical science had a long way to go in the 1920s. Research soon showed that even insulin would not cure the fatal disease; it would only mask the symptoms. Researchers hoped that would be enough to make diabetes a manageable, if chronic, condition. Four decades later, doctors were well aware of the long-range side effects of the "managed" ailment, especially blindness, amputations, kidney failure, and...still...death.

But the general public was mostly unaware of diabetes. These were the days before fast food or mega-markets or even supermarkets, before computers, video games and the internet, before email and cell phones, when televisions aired shows for only part of the day on only three channels—and you got out of your chair to change the channel. In that era, diabetic patients were few and far between, and most of them suffered from "juvenile diabetes," now called Type 1 or early-onset diabetes, or most recently, insulin-dependent diabetes. Type 2 diabetes, the version now nearly epidemic in the United States, was strictly a disease of the elderly in 1961, and not much talked about even at that.

The Type 2 disease, then called adult-onset diabetes, sometimes can be managed with diet and exercise; juvenile diabetes cannot. Diet and exercise are very important, but without insulin, a Type 1 diabetic eventually will waste away. In mid-20th century America, even with insulin, many juvenile diabetics died young.

Blood sugar measurements were inexact at best in the '50s and '60s, and astonishingly infrequent by current standards. Today, someone with diabetes probably checks his or her blood sugar three, four or more times a day, using a tiny almost pain-free needle to prick a finger, squeezing a drop of blood onto a test strip, then taking an additional dose of insulin if the sugar level is higher than recommended. Many diabetics are able to maintain even better blood sugar control thanks to an implanted insulin pump that constantly monitors the chemistry of the blood and automatically releases insulin as needed. New and better personal testing options appear every year. But in the early '60s, patients could not test their own blood. As a new diabetic, Tracy went to the doctor once a month to have his blood tested and to receive the results of the previous month's testing. His mother would re-adjust his diet based on those one-time, month-old blood sugar readings.

"I was a kid. Sometimes I cheated and ate a candy bar," Tracy told me later. "A month later, I would pay the price when the doctor told Mom to cut my diet by so many calories."

The year 1961 had been a good year for Tracy. He began the year playing seventh-grade basketball and soon turned 13. He moved up from Cub Scouts to Boys Scouts, went to Scout camp during the summer, entered eighth grade in the fall and was ready to start every new thing that came along. By December, he had ten merit badges on his Boy Scout sash, from hiking and archery to scholarship and leatherwork. And it was basketball season again.

As Christmas approached, Tracy had no idea there was anything wrong. He did know he was thirstier than usual. He was surprised when he walked to the corner store to quench his thirst, bought two bottles of pop, drank both on the short walk back to the farm, and arrived home just as thirsty as before. He tried to drink milk unobtrusively at meals to avoid his father's notice; eating anything without liquid suddenly seemed like chewing sawdust, he told me years later, remembering those weeks before he or anyone else knew he was diabetic.

During the two-week hospitalization that followed his diagnosis, Tracy first met the realities of the disease he hadn't known he had. He wasn't overly concerned (though no doubt his mother was appalled) when the doctor told him he didn't need to worry about living past 40. "What 13-year-old boy can even imagine that advanced age?" Tracy reflected philosophically, years later. But he was definitely frightened when he experienced his first insulin reaction—though he had no name for the panicky, out-of-control, passing-out feeling that came upon him for the first time around midnight in a darkened hospital room.

Before this, unbeknownst to him, his blood sugar had always been high: bad for his health, responsible for his thirst, connected to the weight loss, but otherwise of no consequence to an active farm boy. Now, as the doctors tried to determine how much insulin it would take to keep his blood sugar at the right level for his body to properly process nutrients, they had overdone it. His body had see-sawed in the opposite direction and now had too little sugar. What he needed, on that dark night in a strange hospital, was sugar: a cookie, orange juice, some sweet cola, even white bread would do. But he didn't know that yet. He only knew something was wrong. He thought he was dying.

The night nurse thought he was a melodramatic teenage boy, at least at first.

Sometime later—perhaps it was almost immediately, though in his memory it was an interminable frightening time—the nurse brought him a small sugar wafer and slowly the panic passed. But it was a long and scary night.

On December 31, the doctors sent him home with needles, syringes, insulin bottles, and a restrictive diet. For Tracy's mother, there were directions for once-daily injections of insulin, for sterilizing the needles and syringes before each use, for carefully weighing and monitoring portions of protein, dairy products, and carbohydrates. For Tracy, there were new routines and a "celebrity" status he did not want: No longer just another farm boy, he believed he would forever be known as "the diabetic kid" at school. It was a distinction he railed against for years.

For Tracy in eighth grade, diabetes became a condition to be disguised, an opponent to be defeated. Only much later was he able to accept the disease as a soul-mate to be managed and endured as long as possible.

The challenge of diabetes would shape his heart and soul, mold his career, and accompany him through a life that did last beyond 40, although that long-ago doctor knew what he was talking about: Dialysis was not a realistic option in 1961, and kidney transplants were still a research dream. Without those life-saving and life-giving procedures, Tracy would indeed have died when he experienced kidney failure in December 1988 at the age of...40.

Tracy first told me about his diabetes in 1983, some months after we had begun getting to know each other. He approached the subject cautiously, even awkwardly.

"I have some health problems," he said, evasively. "You should know." Whatever he was going to tell me was obviously a concern to him.

I waited, now nervous myself. By this time in our relationship, we had met for drinks after work many times, shared a few dinners, gone for some long walks and quite a few drives in the country. I couldn't imagine what could be so wrong, but I found myself holding my breath as he composed his thoughts in silence.

"I have diabetes," he said at last.

I exhaled with relief; and almost with a laugh replied, "Oh! Well, okay. It's not like you have cancer or anything."

It's not like you have cancer or anything. What naiveté.

Two decades later, shortly after Tracy's death, I recalled that conversation to my own doctor. By then, I was a three-year survivor of breast cancer and my dad was fourteen years past his prostate cancer diagnosis. Cancer, I knew, could be beaten. There was no eliminating diabetes. My doctor nodded in sad agreement.

"Yes, Diabetes is sort of like cancer of the whole body."

My doctor was right. I knew it by then. Tracy knew it when he told me; he even predicted that "one day" he might need a kidney transplant. But organ transplants were so rare in the early '80s that the idea that an ordinary person, someone I knew, might have one did not register with me that day. Tracy knew, though, and he tried to be completely honest.

I'll always be grateful that I didn't really "get it" at first. I cherish all my memories, even of the hard times, because we made the most of every moment. But if I had known what was to come, would it have frightened me away? I like to think not, but who can say.

Whether Tracy was chafing against the discipline of diabetes by challenging its every restraint, or whether he was just hot-wired for teenage recklessness, as the '60s progressed he embraced every opportunity to push the limits of adventure, soon aided and abetted by cars and the lure of "3-2 beer" (3.2% alcohol) across the Ohio line.

Tracy's mother—who by now was spending weekdays at nursing school in Ann Arbor, coming home on weekends to cook and clean—later blamed herself for her younger son's "bad boy" high school behavior. "If I'd been there, I would have seen what was happening and kept him in line," she told me.

By comparison with some of today's teen misdeeds, many of Tracy's exploits were not particularly egregious—skipping school to drive to Detroit for auto parts, smoking during basketball season (grounds for sitting out several games), and stumbling drunk to his second floor bedroom on occasional Saturday nights, trying not to wake his parents. There was also drag racing down city streets, knocking off mailboxes once on a country road, and shooting rats at the municipal dump one memorable Saturday night, inadvertently setting the dump on fire.

But these "adventures" had consequences far beyond parental lectures and a couple of school suspensions. Decades later, he would admit that the wild days of his youth, and the accompanying disregard for diabetic control, took a toll on his body that probably could be calculated in months or years.

Long before that, though, he faced consequences of a different kind: The day after graduating from high school in June 1966, he married Judy Neilsen; by October, they were the teenage parents of a baby girl named Cindy. And so, instead of starting freshman year at Michigan State University as he had planned, Tracy started working any job he could find to provide for his new family. He hadn't yet reached his full height, and grew another inch after he was married.

In February 1969, Tracy held the hand of his two-and-a-half-year-old daughter as he blew out the candles on his birthday cake. He was 21 years old.

For me, the 1960s began uneventfully. I finished sixth grade at Academy Avenue School, where I had started as a first grader, with pretty much the same students. But over the next four years, I attended four different schools in two different states, surrounded by new people every fall.

First, two classrooms from another elementary school joined our two classes of sixth-grade graduates. We spent a blissful seventh-grade year isolated in an old wooden 1888 school house. We were the overflow in a growing community. No doubt being relegated to the spartan facilities of Jefferson School was considered a disadvantage; there was no cafeteria, no auditorium, no music or art, and we crossed the street to the YMCA for gym class. But I remember that year, in what amounted to an adolescent incubator, with pure delight. We grew up as fast or slowly as we wanted, entering our teens without pressure to emulate any older kids.

The next year, we moved to the still-new and much larger Central Junior High School, joining kids from many other schools for eighth and ninth grades. I attended my first dance in the Central gym and sprinted down the athletic field with a field hockey stick, hoping I would never come near the ball. I walked away from the brick walls of the school in hushed conversation with my best friend in November that year, 1963, when we were sent home early because President John F. Kennedy had been assassinated.

By the following September, when I would have been at the top of the social heap as a ninth-grader at Central, my family had moved from our New England home in Massachusetts, to a new life forty miles outside of New York City. My father's job as a naval architect for Bethlehem Steel had ended with the closing of the Fore River Shipyard, and he accepted a position as a research professor at his alma mater, Webb Institute of Naval Architecture, on the north shore of Long Island. Our new home, an almost-new house in a newish housing development, was an easy drive from Webb and a short walk from Toaz Junior High School in one direction and Huntington High School in the other. I met an entire new school in ninth grade. A year later, I met classmates from the other junior high, along with all the upperclassmen, when I started at the high school. It might have been daunting to enter a high school of 2,000, in a sophomore class of 700; but by then, though I didn't realize it, I pretty much knew how to make friends and get along in any place I might go.

At the end of eighth grade, shortly after my fourteenth birthday and in anticipation of our move to New York, I hosted my first boy-girl party, a cookout at home, as a sort-of good-bye event. After ten years in the same neighborhood, I had all kinds of friends and they all came. From the broken lawn chairs in our back yard to the battle to keep the lights on in the basement, it was clear that many of them were way ahead of me in their eagerness to jump into every aspect of wild-and-crazy teenage life. I would be a junior in college before I again dared to plan a boy-girl get-together.

In fact, I was aware that leaving Weymouth would be a break with childhood and a move into grown-up life. And I was not happy about it. Unlike many kids, and certainly unlike Tracy, I was in no particular hurry to grow up. I knew that once we moved, I would never again "play horses" with my fellow tomboys, not in this neighborhood or any other. It didn't matter that I had already outgrown that kind of childhood play. What mattered, to the point of tears, was that I wouldn't even have a friend who remembered using our bikes, our legs, and our imaginations to gallop to the far horizons of cowgirl adventure.

And I knew we were not heading in the direction of anything similar to those fantasies.

I had spent a glorious summer, the year before, living on a farm in northern Minnesota with my mother's relatives, caring for my "own" horse, riding through pastures and fields and acres of semi-wild country every day. Sometimes we set aside the western saddles and rode bareback; I practiced for days until I could mount bareback without getting up on a stool: instead, moving back a few steps, then running, jumping, and scrambling up onto my quiet, faithful Buddy. Once on Buddy's broad back, I learned to hold onto his mane as he half-leaped across the creek or hopped over hay bales. I discovered twangy country music that summer and embraced every aspect of my brief time as an "almost farmer's daughter."

"Can't we please move to Minnesota?" I had begged my father, Norman, when I returned home from my country-girl adventure.

"Well, Jennifer, I'm afraid they don't build many ships in Minnesota," he replied.

And, really, I understood. Much as I longed for that life, I was never going to be a farmer's daughter. I would spend one more summer in Minnesota, but my father was a naval architect. He designed ships. We would live near the ocean. And now, we would live near a very big city. We were moving to Long Island.

But I never questioned the move to New York, never considered pleading to stay behind; our family was too strong. We would go together, even my older sister who arrived at our new home the night before starting senior year in a new high school, after spending the summer waitressing in New Hampshire.

The move changed all of us, and the changes were all positive, we realized later. During the first year, our family bonded in unexpected ways. None of us knew anyone at first, so we went to the new James Bond movie together; picnicked on various Long Island beaches together; visited all the tourist landmarks in Manhattan together, taking in the view from the Empire State Building and climbing to the top of the Statue of Liberty. And we went to the New York World's Fair together—a lot. The World's Fair, symbolized by the Unisphere that still stands as a landmark next to the then-brand-new Shea Stadium, began its two-summer run on Long Island just as we became New Yorkers. My mother, Barbara, worried that we (or she) would be lonely in our new home state, so she encouraged relatives, friends, everyone we knew to come visit us those first two summers. I went to the World's Fair seventeen times.

In today's era of instant news from all points on the globe and push-button communication with anyone anywhere anytime, it's hard to imagine the impact of a World's Fair back then; but for me, the 1964-65 fair was a dizzying immersion into all kinds of new ideas, strange tastes and far-away cultures, from Belgian waffles to Philippine wood carving, from the social history of electricity to the Mormon concept of the hereafter to the information-processing powers of the computer, and lots of stops in between.

The move to Long Island broadened my horizons in other

ways, too. I heard new accents in my neighborhood, met students of different colors and backgrounds at school, shared friends' Hanukkah plans as my family prepared for Christmas.

Then there was New York City itself. My dad enjoyed a bucolic drive to work at Webb, but many of my friends' fathers headed into Manhattan each morning, driving on the crammed Long Island Expressway or parking at the town railroad station for a train commute; either way, going "into the City" was accepted as a normal part of life, and not just for parents. Friends of mine took the train independently to attend weekend Hebrew classes in New York. One of my first dates was a trip by train into NYC to visit the Museum of Modern Art.

Thanks to a progressive school system and adventurous high school teachers, I enjoyed amazing school-day field trips into New York, whole classes of us crowding onto the Long Island Railroad, changing trains in Jamaica, then catching the subway to attend plays and concerts, visit temples and cathedrals, examine art and architecture. I saw Hal Holbrook portray "Mark Twain Tonight." Watched wide-eyed from the Lincoln Center balcony as the New York City Ballet danced "Don Giovanni." Was overwhelmed by the rapid-fire wit and repartee of Tom Stoppard's new play, "Rosencrantz and Guildenstern are Dead."

Forty-and-more years later, I wonder if any public school today would accept the risks involved in those late-sixties excursions—and I thank my lucky stars that my school did. Those exuberant, eye-opening, mind-expanding day trips showed me how much there was to learn, to explore, to enjoy in the world of people and ideas—and how easy it was to get up and go. From then on, I would know that travel was possible, going to new places was fun, and the world was waiting.

Although I chose a rural campus when I went off to college in Middlebury, Vermont, I comfortably traveled through New York

City by train and bus on my occasional trips back and forth. On Christmas vacation and spring break at home, I almost always spent some time in the "Big Apple," going to a concert or visiting museums—MOMA for modern art, the Guggenheim for interesting exhibits in a circular setting, the Whitney for American art, the massive Metropolitan Museum of Art for anything as long as you had the time.

After college graduation I surprised even myself by choosing, finally, to live in New York City.

By the early 1970s, Tracy's and my lives could hardly have been more different.

He was a husband and a father in a small rural town, a political conservative, and an apprentice automotive designer with a union card and big business dreams. He built remote-control airplanes for fun. Raced motorcycles on weekends at fair grounds and racetracks all around the Midwest. Re-built car engines in his garage—or sometimes on the living room floor.

I was a single woman in America's biggest city, working in public relations by day and taking life-drawing classes in the evening. I shared an upscale apartment with girlfriends who joined me in sampling an endless array of ethnic restaurants and all the excitement New York had to offer—from Bette Midler and Broadway to the Brooklyn Bridge and the Staten Island Ferry; from the New York Philharmonic to modern dance and inscrutable performance art. I even rented a horse once and spent an hour riding on the bridle paths around Central Park.

Mine was an exciting and stimulating life, but lonely, too, sometimes, even in that crowded city. I rode the subway late at night, went out for fresh bagels at 2 a.m., and began longing for something like the American family dream. And that, as much as academic inspiration, led me from New York to the Midwest for graduate school, journalism, art reviewing and finally college administration.

But love would take its time.

As I wrote much later, in an update for my twenty-fifth college reunion: "Who knew that Mr. Right would turn out to be a bird-hunter, business man and motorcycle racer?"

I kissed my share of good-hearted frogs before finding my prince.

A Wink and a Smile

December 1988. Toledo, Ohio. Late afternoon on a grey and darkening day.

I walk slowly, carefully, deliberately placing one foot in front of the other as I move down the ramped hallway from the parking garage toward the main building of Toledo Hospital. It is unfamiliar territory. Not just this place but hospitals in general. My mind wanders nervously. I can't remember ever being in a hospital before. Not since I had my tonsils out. But I can't really remember that; I was only five.

That was thirty-three years ago.

Lost in memory, I glance up from my feet. A fleeting sense of recognition stops me, and I turn to gaze at the backs of the elderly couple who just passed me going the other way, making their way back up to the garage. He is a tall man in suspenders; she is shorter, with a purse hanging on her arm.

His parents, I wonder? I've only met them once.

Should I call to them?

But the moment has passed. I move on down the ramp.

Emerging into the hospital lobby, my insides tighten. I want to turn around, go back. You just drove two-and-a-half hours to get here, I tell myself silently. You can't go back.

I ask at the desk: seventh floor, elevator around the corner.

Can anyone see how lost I feel? (Do I have any inkling how familiar this will all become?)

Seven floors up, the desk nurse is breezy and matter-of-fact. "He's in dialysis. Right down the hall. You can go in."

'You can go in.'

Can I, I wonder? Can I do this?

I stop in front of the double doors with no windows, and take a deep breath. Then push the door open into a startlingly bright white room. Beds and chairs are paired with blocky machines covered with dials and electronic monitors. I scan the room, find him on the right, and focus. He is on a hospital recliner, not unlike a chaise lounge on someone's back porch. But a white blanket covers him up to his bare chest. Tubes come out of his chest, just below his left shoulder, tethering him to a rhythmic humming machine.

He turns his head, and sees me. Crinkling his eyes, blue even from a distance, he smiles his crooked grin. Then he winks.

And just like that—magic!—my world is right again.

I exhale at last, smiling back.

This is still Tracy, my Tracy. He is still himself. Tubes and hospital gowns and dialysis—whatever that turns out to be—will not change him. Or us.

Of course, I can do this, I realize without thinking. Why did I ever worry? As long as he is still himself, we will be okay. It is all clear to me now: with him I can handle anything. We can handle it. We will do it together.

That simple, world-altering exchange repeated itself many times. A wink challenging worry. A crooked smile inviting laughter. Love and trust overcoming fear and uncertainty.

About a year after that hospital visit, Tracy and I walked into his Adrian, Michigan, apartment to find the phone ringing. It was Friday night about 10 o'clock, the day after Thanksgiving, and we had just arrived back from the dialysis clinic. I was visiting for the holiday weekend from my home near Columbus, Ohio, several hours away. We had cooked a big turkey in his tiny kitchen the day before. Today, late in the afternoon, we had driven the forty-five minutes to Toledo; I went Christmas shopping while he spent three hours hooked up to the dialysis machine, as he had done three times a week all year, ever since that magic wink.

Three hours was a long time to be stuck in a chair—but not so long when you considered that all of the blood would leave his body, travel through a maze of tubes and filters that cleaned the blood as well as science knew how, then travel back into his body. It usually took me about a half hour to donate a pint of blood; and most of us have between five and eight pints of blood in our bodies. Looked at that way, three hours didn't seem excessive. But three hours, plus start-up and shut-down, plus travel time, three times a week without fail: that is a big commitment. That commitment runs your life. Ask any dialysis patient.

Tracy was in the minority in the dialysis community: He still worked full-time, running a manufacturing company. And he was alone, having ended a long marriage almost two years earlier. He drove himself to the dialysis clinic in Toledo, a forty-five minute trip after work three days a week, and drove home again, arriving after 10:00 p.m. to collapse into bed in the state of sick exhaustion that always followed that blood-out-of-body experience.

But this was Thanksgiving and we were together. We had the whole weekend. Tracy was wiped out from the Friday night dialysis, but we were happy, laughing as we came through the door to find the phone ringing. Tracy picked up the receiver.

"Hello? Yes?" He grew serious, listening intently.

"Alright," he said finally. "We'll be there." He hung up the phone, then turned to me.

"There's a kidney available. They want me to come in for testing. Right now."

Back to Toledo. A different hospital. We made our way for the first time to the Medical College of Ohio Hospital. In the MCO waiting room, late at night, we met one of the other candidates for the kidney, a young woman who sat with her husband. Several candidates were tested as possible matches for each organ available for transplant.

The doctors sent us home in the wee hours of the morning, to wait for the results, with instructions not to eat.

Tracy spent most of Saturday lying on the couch, doing as little as possible in order to keep his body from using up the sugar it had from the day before, sucking occasional lifesavers and doing his best to maintain the balance between insulin and sugar without actually eating. The luscious leftovers of our Thanksgiving feast went untouched.

As the day dragged on, Tracy became increasingly depressed, certain the kidney would go to the young woman we'd met who was so healthy, not yet even on dialysis. Twice before, he'd been called for testing when a kidney became available; both times we rushed back from vacation only to find he was not the chosen one. By now, dialysis had taken a toll on his body, eating away at his well-being even as it made life possible. The vigorous young woman would obviously be a better candidate for surgery, he reasoned. With each passing hour, he was more convinced that this kidney, too, would pass him by.

Then, late in the afternoon, almost evening, the phone rang. Tracy answered. "Hello?" he said tentatively... *Yes!* We notified family and headed back to Toledo. We were excited, scared, and full of hope.

Kidney failure is one of the most common side effects of long-term diabetes. Over enough time, excess sugar in the blood eventually damages just about everything in the body; but the kidneys are often among the first casualties. The kidneys—most of us get two to start with, but all you need is one—are the body's cleaning system. They filter toxins from the blood and send them out in the urine. As the kidneys begin to fail, kidney function declines, urine output diminishes and the poisons remain in the body, accumulating in the blood and showing up in unhealthy measurements of things like BUN and creatinine.

Dialysis does a pretty good cleaning job, but it is an imperfect substitute for a kidney. While removing the fluid that builds up when a body more or less stops peeing, dialysis sifts most—but not all—of the bad stuff out of the blood. Ironically, some minerals that healthy people seek as nutritional additives become toxic enemies to dialysis patients. Potassium, for example, is important for muscles and nerves (it helps most people avoid leg cramps) and also for proper functioning of the heart and the kidneys. But potassium is one thing dialysis cannot fully remove from the blood, so it builds up; and too much potassium will stop the heart. Eat the wrong things as a dialysis patient—things you previously thought were really good for you like fresh fruit and vegetables, dairy products, even lean meat—and potassium builds up to dangerously high levels. Finding the right things to eat can be very difficult. Diet becomes a critical part of daily health care for all renal patients, especially for those who are also diabetic.

End-stage renal disease—the first diagnosis of trouble—had put Tracy onto a strict diet several years earlier, severely restricting his consumption of protein, dairy products, salt, and carbohydrate. He was already used to the restrictions of diabetes; so, with his kidneys functioning at about 20% of normal (at 10% dialysis would be required), he embraced the new limitations with stoicism and his trademark wry humor: "Current course of action is a very restricted diet," he wrote to me at the time, in a letter from Michigan to Ohio. "Everything is measured. Salt, protein, potassium and sugar levels have to be kept very low. This removes all edible substances. I am now living on salt-free low protein bread (also called cardboard)." He determined to think of food only as nutrition, not as a focus for fun or celebration.

Even so, he was only able to slow, not stop, the deterioration of the kidneys.

By the time we were ready to share each other's office Christmas parties, declaring to our separate worlds that we were a couple, Tracy was skeletally thin, trying to eat as little as possible. Still, even "good" food—food that met his dietary requirements and tasted good when it went down—often came back up. Tracy was very good at hiding his difficulties, though, and I didn't realize what was happening at first.

The weekend of his Christmas party, I did notice that he was very skinny, each rib showing like a mini mountain range on his narrow chest, and I was startled by the image that came into my mind: Michelangelo's Pieta, Mary cradling the dead and emaciated Christ. I shook the picture from my mind, promised silently never to complain about gaining weight again, and went back to getting ready for the Aidco office party. Tracy's response when I emerged from the bedroom in a new black velvet dress—"Oh, Jennifer, you look stunning!"—swept all other thought from my mind; I was oblivious to anything but my own happiness for the rest of the evening.

A week later, he joined me for the Ohio Wesleyan holiday festivities: a cocktail party hosted by a faculty friend followed by the University Christmas Ball. This time, even in my excitement, I recognized that Tracy was hardly eating. And excusing himself frequently...to throw up, I figured out later. By the next day, I understood how bad things were. I offered to drive him back to Toledo, take him to a hospital or to a doctor. But after another bout of vomiting, he was "fine," he said; he could handle the drive by himself. He went home alone. Two nights later, he called with the new diagnosis: renal failure. The kidneys were done for. He was in the hospital. He would start dialysis that evening.

The following day, I drove to Toledo, visiting him that first time in a hospital.

Over the next year, his world revolved around the three-times-a-week sessions at a Toledo dialysis clinic. He spent Monday, Wednesday and Friday evenings hooked up to a machine. Tracy's professional involvement with hydraulics and machine design made him curious about the mechanics of the process, making him friends with the technicians who maintained the equipment. His upbeat attitude made him a favorite with the nursing staff, as well as the other patients, all of whom welcomed me when I drove up from Columbus for Friday night "dialysis dates" to kick off my weekend visits.

For a while, dialysis seemed manageable; inconvenient, sure, but not as much of a problem as we had worried. Midway through that year, when Tracy was still quite vigorous, he even rearranged his dialysis so we could schedule a weekend rendezvous on Jekyll Island in Georgia.

But as Thanksgiving neared, it was clear that his overall health was declining. He had less and less energy; and the drive home after dialysis became more and more difficult.

For those awaiting organ transplants, holiday weekends are, in a macabre way, a time of heightened promise: Just as summertime puts more motorcycles on the road (and bikers, especially those who ride without helmets, end up providing many cadaver organs for transplantation), jubilant holiday celebrations put more than the usual number of drunk drivers on the road. Sadly, highway accidents are one of the biggest sources of donated organs. One family's fatal tragedy provides the miracle of life for another family, sometimes several or even many families.

On this Thanksgiving weekend in 1989, one family somewhere in central Ohio mourned a great loss, while at the Medical College of Ohio Hospital in Toledo at least two other families prayed for a second chance at a healthy life. The donor's two kidneys arrived; and late that Saturday night, Tracy and a young guitar-playing college athlete each began trying to live with a new organ.

It was not a smooth process.

A few days later, the young man's mother wept in the waiting room; for whatever reason, despite the doctors' best efforts and intensive treatment with immune-suppressing drugs, her son's body had rejected the new kidney. We tried to comfort her with our eyes; but we did not speak with the mother. What could we say? We were afraid of jinxing our own patient's prospects.

And so we waited. And waited.

With the help of the drugs, Tracy's body seemed to be accepting the new organ. But nothing was happening. Many times each hour I glanced surreptitiously at the "pee bag" hanging from his bed, but there was no urine flow. Tracy went back to dialysis while still at the hospital. After a few days, he went home, and continued the three-times-weekly dialysis drives to Toledo, but now I or his sister or his mother drove him—driving was forbidden during post-transplant recovery.

The doctors were evasive, not promising anything but not giving up. Sometimes the process of "harvesting" an organ, or the circumstances that lead up to it, leave the organ "traumatized" for a while, they said. It might be "sleeping."

Just wait, they said.

Three weeks after the transplant, on a snowy non-dialysis day just before Christmas, Tracy and I attended the closing on a house we had bid on before Thanksgiving. On doctor's orders, he wore a surgical mask to protect him from any airborne cold or flu germs. We made sport of the mask—I called him Zorro and Dr. Zorba—and we tried not to think about the successful but apparently useless transplant. We focused on the future: a house and a new life together.

"Sorry about the mask," Tracy said to the group assembled around the long conference table. "Don't worry—it's for my protection, not yours." The bankers chuckled.

Midway through the process of umpteen signatures, with legal documents strewn all across the table, Tracy pushed his chair back and asked, through the mask, "Can you tell me where to find the men's room?"

What? I stared after him as he went down the hall. Tracy never needed a restroom. His urine output had been minimal for months, first because of kidney failure and then dialysis. I was the one who asked for restrooms, not Tracy.

When he returned, there was a twinkle in his eyes and behind the mask, I was pretty sure there was a smile. Settling back into his chair, he looked straight at me. And then he winked.

The kidney was finally awake!

"Congratulations! I hear you got urine for Christmas!" another kidney transplant recipient wrote in her Christmas card. Yes, indeed! It was gold, frankincense and myrrh all wrapped up together. For the first time in my life, I did not spend Christmas with my parents, choosing instead to stay in Michigan with the man I would marry seven months later and the girls who would become my daughters, too.

The message on my Christmas card that year was straightforward: "On Christmas and every morning, the best gift is a new day. Open it with joy." In my simple line drawing, the colored-pencil sunrise through the window outshined all the gaily wrapped presents under the tree.

Dialysis and a kidney transplant were only the first of many scary unknowns Tracy and I would face together. Hospitals became all too familiar—their waiting rooms, gift shops, and cafeterias all places where I sought solace or diversion while he tackled one medical challenge after another, all related to the diabetes he had lived with for thirty, then forty, years. But always—on an ER gurney hooked up to an IV, through the unpredictable waiting period before each new surgery, or in an ICU bed with a breathing tube silencing his voice—always, when I needed it most, Tracy gave me that gift of love and reassurance: a wink to banish worry, a quirky smile to combat fear. Each time it made me love him more.

A good attitude doesn't change a bad diagnosis. Facts are facts. But the ability to wink at fate and smile in the darkness makes it a lot easier to get through hard times.

It was a magic we would make often.

Finding Our Way
Words and a Wedding

July 7, 2010. Wednesday. It's going to be another scorcher here in southeast Michigan.

I'll be at work today, crafting the words for this year's Homecoming brochure. Also correcting some words already sent out to some of our reunion classes: One alumna emailed me yesterday to point out that my recent letter had seesawed between October 1, 2010, and October 10, 2009. I pride myself on careful proofreading, so this will be a day of professional humility and damage control. Mea culpa.

In among this day's wordsmithing tasks, I'll daydream about another day, and other words, carefully and lovingly crafted twenty years ago.

July 7, 1990, was a picture-perfect summer Saturday in Maine, gloriously clear and bright, warm but not hot—comfortable for the long-sleeved satin gown my mother had designed and made for her own wedding forty-four years earlier.

On this day, Tracy and I—with all four of our parents, all four of our siblings and their spouses, his (now *our*) three daughters and one granddaughter, plus nieces, nephews, aunts, uncles and friends there to cheer us—held hands in an old white meetinghouse in the coastal town of Pemaquid and said, "I do." Two words—and we became a family. I became a wife, a mother, and a grandmother. It was a wonderful day and the best wedding I've ever attended. (I wish every bride could feel that way.)

Waiting outside in the sun before the ceremony, while everyone else entered the meetinghouse, my father and I smiled at each other. Then, on the narrow winding road a few feet away, several bicyclists pedaled by; the last called out an exuberant "L'chaim!" as he passed. The Jewish celebration toast: "To life!" It was perfectly appropriate and I've always been grateful to that nameless cheery young man. Yes, indeed: "L'chaim!"

Not much more than half an hour later, Tracy and I walked back down the aisle, emerging from the meetinghouse into the bright afternoon as our ninety-plus guests, tentatively at first and then with enthusiasm, sang along with the string quartet: "Zip a dee doo dah, zip a dee ay! My, oh my, what a wonderful day! Plenty of sunshine coming my way. Zip a dee doo dah, zip a dee ay!"

Yes, indeed. I remember every moment of the ceremony.

Turning the corner to start down the main aisle, holding onto my father's arm, seeing Tracy struggling with tears, and smiling to him in encouragement. Reaching the front of the meeting house. Turning to face our dearly beloveds seated in groups in the old-fashioned pew boxes. Taking Tracy's hand.

The words we heard and said.

My sister reading from Anne Morrow Lindbergh's *Gift from the Sea*: "A good relationship has a pattern like a dance...now (the partners are) arm in arm, now face to face, now back to back... moving to the same rhythm... Security in a relationship lies neither in looking back to what it was in nostalgia, nor forward to what it might be in dread or anticipation, but living in the present...and accepting it as it is now."

My brother playing the banjo and singing a simple Bill Staines tune: "Loving you is oh so easy. Loving you is oh so fine. Even on a cold gray morning, we can see the sunlight shine."

Mary, our minister, reminding everyone that a good marriage enhances rather than diminishes the individuality of the partners and that a wedding is more than the marriage of a man and woman: "It is also the union of families and friends" and "some people are very fortunate and have many families."

Inviting our daughters and granddaughter to stand with us and celebrate the start of a new family.

I remember it all as if it were yesterday, and not just because my brother-in-law unobtrusively videotaped it for us, in what turned out to be a most precious gift.

Tracy and I wrote our wedding ceremony together, over several weeks, in long reflective sessions on our back porch. We chose the words carefully, thoughtfully. Mary, the minister, had provided several traditional wedding rituals for us to review, and gave us wide flexibility in what to include and how to say it. We spent hours, especially, discussing our vows. What was this commitment we were making? What did we want it to be?

Finally, on that day in Maine, we came "freely and happily" to marry each other. Along with loving and comforting, we promised "to learn and grow" together, and to be honest and faithful, "in good times and when life is hard."

We vowed to "love and to cherish, to respect and encourage, to help and ask for help, for richer or poorer, in sickness and in health, in joy and in sadness, as long as we both shall live."

We gave each other rings, whose sparkle would remind us "to laugh well and to love deeply."

The words were important to us, not just in that ceremony or on that day, but every day. We remembered the words we spoke, and we talked about them in the years that followed. It was interesting, in fact, what proved to be most important as time passed: Loving and cherishing, for us, were all about learning and growing, individually and together; respecting and encouraging; helping, and asking for help.

The words were important. And we talked about them.

That, in fact, was the heart of our relationship.

Words brought us together in the first place. Words and circumstance.

Ours was not a case of love at first sight. It is true we were drawn to each other almost immediately, but it was not physical attraction or animal magnetism or emotional fireworks, though soon enough all those things intensified what we felt. But on our first meeting, a January evening in 1983, it was words that kindled an instant connection: words, ideas and thoughtful conversation.

It happened like this. At a time when all of my 30-something friends often regrouped after work at a local watering hole, I and my best pal, an artist, met for a drink before heading home. We both worked at Adrian College in southeast Michigan. At some point, her boyfriend (who was also my friend and my former boss) arrived unexpectedly with his new friend (and new boss) from a local manufacturing firm. They joined us, he on one side of the table with my artist pal, his friend/boss on the other side with me.

As the couple across from us immediately locked eyes, lips and emotions, Tracy and I turned to face one another and asked politely about each other's work. I don't recall the specifics of the conversation, but I clearly remember turning to face him, slightly embarrassed, and initiating conversation about something other than the kissing couple across the table.

And I remember turning back sometime later as our two friends rose to leave; I was surprised to realize how much time had passed. Apparently, we had excluded them just as effectively from our conversation as they excluded us from theirs.

In any case, neither Tracy nor I made a move to follow them.

Sometime after that, Tracy said—and this I remember precisely: "Would it be inappropriate to ask if you would like to get something to eat?"

The formality and shy politeness of the question—so in contrast with the prevailing ways of the world—delighted me, even though I knew it probably was not appropriate. Because even though he did not wear a wedding ring, I knew he was married. My old boss had mentioned *his* interesting new boss a few times before this.

But Tracy and I were just talking. Just talking. That's all. Nothing was "happening," I reasoned, and it had been a long time since I'd enjoyed such engaging conversation.

"Yes, that would be nice," I said. "But it has to be some place that takes credit cards. I'm all out of cash."

A hint of surprise crossed his face; he was old-fashioned enough, I realized later, to assume that of course the invitation meant he would pay; but I was "liberated" enough to assume absolutely not. We agreed on a destination and left in our separate cars.

I arrived at the restaurant and found a booth. And then I waited. And waited. And began mentally kicking myself for no longer having any accurate instincts about men. He seemed like a genuinely nice person, but how long should I wait, I wondered, before concluding he wasn't coming? I was about to leave when he appeared, apologizing profusely. He'd been running on empty and stopped for gas. (Did he also call home to say he'd be late? I always wondered.)

The conversation over hamburgers was more personal than earlier. We told each other where we had traveled (he: Mexico,

South America, England; me: France, Greece and Afghanistan) and how old we were (he: 34, I: 32). And then we left.

As we walked up the sidewalk toward our cars, we agreed it had been nice meeting each other. That was it. So long.

Nice guy, I thought. Too bad he's married. Oh well.

It was weeks later at another after-work gathering, this time with a big group of colleagues, when my friend and his boss again walked into the bar. As a former co-worker, my friend knew everyone in the group and he immediately led Tracy in our direction.

For me, there was a moment of startled recognition, and then delight, when Tracy made a beeline for the empty chair by me. Or perhaps he pulled one up. Over gin-and-tonics, once again we talked. And again, we were the last two seated, still talking after everyone else had left. We said goodbye in the parking lot. A casual and totally proper, "Nice to see you again."

It continued like that. Every few weeks or so, we ran into each other, always in a bar, always with friends, always by chance (or so I told myself). And each time we were drawn together by what seemed an endless capacity for shared words and mutual curiosity.

"What is there to worry about? We don't plan it and we're always in a group," I rationalized when bothered by uncomfortable thoughts. I had always been very clear, with myself and others, that it was not right to play with a married man; there were too many other lives at stake.

"These are not dates," I told myself. "What can happen?"

And nothing did "happen," not in the romance-novel sense, for a good long while. In retrospect, of course, it was clear something definitely was going on. We had crossed no lines, but running into each other had become much more than a casual surprise. A song from an old musical echoed in my mind: "You fly down the street, on the chance that you'll meet—and you meet, not really by chance," sings Anna in "The King and I," a show I'd been in back in high school. That's just how it was now. We didn't plan it, but we sure gave it every opportunity to happen.

About four-and-a-half months after our first meeting, Tracy and I once more met "by chance" and ended up alone at a bar table, the last stragglers of what had been a large group. It was May. I was wearing a green satin blouse and a tan skirt. We were laughing and talking, same as always. I was telling him about my father's work in naval architecture, which piqued his own interest in mechanical engineering. I leaned toward him, laughing, to make a point.

And then a woman approached the table, focused on Tracy.

I remember thinking, fleetingly, that her manner was a bit presumptuous, rude even. She ignored me completely. Then, maybe one second after she stepped up, it hit me: This was Tracy's wife. After a few moments, she left. Tracy apologized. And then he left, too.

I sat for several minutes stunned, frozen in place. I could no longer pretend that nothing could happen. It might be "just" words, but no matter. The words were important. And something had happened.

For a while, there would be no more talking.

Don't get involved with a married man. Just don't. That had always been my rule. In my New York City days, and in summers working at an artists' workshop in Maine, I had watched women flirt and play with other people's husbands; it was always a bad idea. First of all, it was cheating. Second of all, there were so many other people to consider—especially kids. Finally, it never ended well. It was wrong, plain and simple.

You just don't do it. That was my mantra.

But after a long silence, I was the one who spoke first. I knew I shouldn't. I did anyway. Very deliberately. It was not by accident.

It was four months after that abrupt ending. One September day a little after 5 p.m., I picked up the phone and dialed the number of the office where my old boss now worked, knowing he would not be there. He had a standing commitment on Wednesdays and always left early. But Tracy, I knew, usually worked late. I would play dumb and ask for my friend, hoping that Tracy himself picked up the phone—and that I would recognize his voice. He did. And I did.

I pretended it was completely by chance.

Why did I break my own rule? I don't even remember anymore. But not long after we hung up, the two of us sat side by side on bar stools, meeting for the first time by design.

"I wanted to call you but I wasn't sure you'd want to hear from me," Tracy admitted.

Communication was simpler—it would not do to say "more innocent"—thirty years ago. There were no cell phones, no smart phones. No email or texting. No Facebook or YouTube or Twitter. And no ever-present cameras taking instant pictures to send or share or post to the world.

For a man and a woman in the early '80s, drawn together again and again by words and by that electric something that came through the words, there was only the telephone (which rang in one place and stayed there), the U.S. mail, and face-to-face conversation, then as now the gold standard of communication.

But that fall, as the days grew shorter and darkness fell earlier and earlier, there was a new kind of communication, through hands touching across the table and lips meeting in wishful goodbyes as we leaned against his car or mine, oblivious to the wintry night air.

For a long time, those parking lot embraces in thick winter coats were as far as it went. Physically, anyway. But emotionally, and you might say intellectually, we were all in. Meeting for a drink (now in more out-of-the-way places) or for a walk outside of town, he talked about his daughters, challenges at work, books he was reading, how he had grown up, both before and after marriage. I talked about my family in New England, challenges in my job, books, friends, the Camp Fire Group I was leading, the things I hoped for in life.

Eventually, though, words were not enough.

I reflected, later, on the irony of our relationship: Instead of jumping into bed on a first date like so many other people, we had done things in the "right" order. We got to know each other very well, long before sharing a kiss. And then we kissed a long time before going any further. Eventually, too far gone in desire, we made love.

That was how it was supposed to work, I thought.

But not when one of us was already married.

Despite the obvious adultery of the situation, I never thought of our relationship as an affair. To me, an "affair" was something cheap and tawdry: superficial, temporary, an irresponsible dalliance.

That's not us, I thought, when reading the postcards Tracy sent from his travels, or writing the letters I sent to him at his office under a literary pseudonym, or dialing his work number at 5:30 in the afternoon.

That's not us, I thought, hanging up the phone from one of his calls, realizing that the day was suddenly a very good one, no matter what else had happened. No, that's not us, I thought, as we kissed goodnight in the shadows of yet another parking lot or held hands on Michigan Avenue during meet-you-in-Chicago weekends.

This is not an affair. This is special and real and honest.

Not entirely honest, said the one person whose opinion I could not refute.

Just as I now looked for Tracy's white Chevrolet Impala in every parking lot in town, his wife looked for my car, though I never learned how she had identified it or me. She found me one Saturday, in a laundromat folding towels.

I had just folded my fourth bath towel carefully in thirds the long way, then in half the other way, when I looked up: Judy stood across the laundry table from me, silently waiting.

"Oh! Oh..." What more could I say?

Glancing past her, through the laundry windows, I saw her blue van. I knew her car by then, too. I looked back at her, then down at my towels, then back at her again. I smoothed the half-folded towel, over and over again.

"Once you knew he was married, why did you keep seeing him?" Judy looked straight at me. I stared back, mute.

Still smoothing the towel, I finally said, "It's always been an honest relationship. We've always been open and honest."

"No," she said back to me. "Not completely honest." She was crying as she walked back to the blue van.

She sat in the driver's seat for a few minutes before pulling out of the parking lot.

I stood without moving for a long time, my hands frozen in place on the pile of towels. Finally, I gathered the laundry, folded and unfolded, into a basket and drove to my apartment.

Her words were important, too.

An affair was superficial, irresponsible and cheap, I thought. That's not us. But a confrontation between the wife and the lover over towels in a laundromat? That seemed to meet the definition.

I tried hard to find someone else to love.

Finally, when I could foresee a lifetime spent scanning parking lots looking for Tracy's car, I found another job and moved to another state. The day before leaving town, I went by myself for lunch at an eatery near Tracy's office. As I had secretly hoped, our paths crossed one last time.

Twice, Tracy had tried to walk away from his marriage. Twice, we had tried to stop seeing each other. We had broken things off for the third and final time eight months earlier, but we still talked occasionally. Now we sat at an outdoor picnic table with our fast food, both of us sad.

"If I stayed here," I said, "it wouldn't mean things were going to work out for us. The fact that I'm leaving is no guarantee that things can never work out for us, either."

But we knew it was a lot less likely.

"If you are ever available, you come find me," I said finally, struggling to hold myself together. "Don't *not* look for me because you think I'll be settled in a new life or I won't want to see you. You *find* me."

We went to our separate cars, as we had so often before, this time both wiping away tears. The next day I drove off to a new life in central Ohio, still crying.

I threw myself into the challenges of my new job as director of public relations at Ohio Wesleyan University. I made friends. I dated several fellows and tried to be excited about it. Once in a while, Tracy would call me, sometimes during the day at work, sometimes at home in the evening; as it had always been, a call from Tracy magically turned any day into a good one.

He wrote when he was diagnosed with kidney disease, telling me about the lousy diet he now lived on; and then, a year after my move, he asked me to meet him for Saturday afternoon coffee in Findlay, Ohio, midway between our two homes. It was a bittersweet meeting, but by then I had built a strong brick wall around my heart for protection. When we said goodbye in Findlay, I thought: "This is really it. He'll never leave his marriage. He thinks this kidney thing would be too much to burden me with. And maybe he doesn't have the courage to try." I put another brick in the wall.

But I was wrong, as it turned out.

A few months later, he sent me pictures of his daughters on Christmas morning. Then, early in January, he came to see me, having scheduled a stop in Columbus during a business trip. "My New Year's resolution is to see you as often as I can," he said.

For a moment, I couldn't speak. Then I struggled to get the words out. "I... I don't think that's a good idea."

The brick wall shook, but held.

He called several weeks later. "I'm about to change my whole life," he said. "I need to know if there's a chance for us."

My voice shook when I finally answered. "I can't tell you that," I said, my hand on the receiver shaking even more. "You can't make your decision based on me. You have to do what's right for you, what will make your life better—with the girls and with yourself. Independent of me. This can't be about me."

The words were so hard. And so scary. I hung up and wept.

A few weeks later, for the third time, he moved out of the house he had bought with such high hopes a couple of years before we met. This time, he knew it was for good—and he did all the things he had not done the first two times. He sat down with each of his daughters to tell them, individually, what he was doing and how much he loved them. He made formal arrangements to support Judy and the girls. He signed a two-year lease on an apartment; and bought some furniture including a hide-a-bed so the girls could visit. He purchased drapes and a coffee-maker. He told his parents and his sister and brother.

Finally, I agreed to meet him at a tavern in Michigan's Irish Hills, while visiting friends for the weekend. In a sign, perhaps, that we were both in a fragile place and dealing with serious issues, we each separately ordered club soda. No gin and tonics this time—nothing to muddy our minds. We talked for a long time. The first brick fell out of the wall protecting my heart. I felt it fall, almost literally.

We began to see each other—carefully, discretely—sometimes at my place, sometimes somewhere in between, eventually at his place. At first, it was once a month, then every three weeks. We went bird watching and bicycling, visited wineries and art galleries, went to basketball games and plays.

One by one, the bricks fell, letting light and air into my heart.

In November, Tracy took me to meet Sarah and Michelle, whom we still called Shelly. It was a brief but unhurried introduction at his parents' farm, where I also met Vohne and Florence for the first time. Soon afterward, he was diagnosed with kidney failure, and began balancing dialysis treatments along with weekend visits from the two girls. (His oldest, Cindy, was married with a child of her own.)

At Christmas time, I made stockings for Tracy to hang in his apartment to help him celebrate the holidays with his daughters and his toddler granddaughter, Alexandria. I sent a small gift for each of the girls, but I went home to Maine for Christmas. After that fall visit at the farm, I did not see Tracy's daughters again until the next summer.

We planned our visits carefully. First, Tracy and I went to Indiana so I could meet his oldest daughter, Cindy, and two-year-old Alex face-to-face. Then we spent a day at Wamplers Lake with Sarah and Michelle, picnicking and swimming and getting to know each other. The girls and I still laugh about that afternoon, when 12-year-old Sarah confronted me with every question she could think of. As Tracy sat on the beach, watching the three of us play in the lake, Sarah swam over underwater, again and again, popping her head up and peppering me with questions: "How do you feel about being a stepmom? Are you going to marry my Dad? Has he asked you to marry him? If he did ask, would you say yes? Do you think Dad is handsome? Do you love him? How do you feel about us?" She was not angry; just nosy in a good-hearted way. Just curious.

I splashed around in confusion, unprepared, trying to answer and not answer, to be honest but not any more than necessary. I bobbed underwater myself a few times, needing a moment to think. After all, the words were important, hers and mine. I wanted the girls to know I would always be willing to talk, even about awkward subjects.

"I don't know the answer to that yet," I said several times that day, usually laughing. And that was true; I really didn't.

The day at the lake was a good beginning. And before long, the wall around my heart was gone. I didn't need it anymore.

By the end of the year, Tracy had his new kidney and we spent our first Christmas together. Soon after Valentine's Day, we called my parents.

"Mom," I said. "I was just wondering.

"Do you think I might fit into your wedding dress?"

The greatest disappointment in Tracy's life was that he was unable to fulfill his wedding vows to Judy, unable to live at home with Sarah and Shelly as they grew through adolescence and into the teen years. He regretted that to the end. I knew and accepted that, and even loved that about him, knowing it in no way lessened his love for me.

But words mattered. So when the time came, we labored carefully over our own wedding vows.

Fourteen years later, I thought often about our vows as Tracy lay in bed at the OSU Medical Center. We had promised "to learn and grow" together. I, Jennifer, had taken Tracy "to be my husband, to love and to cherish, to respect and to encourage, to help and to ask for help, for richer, for poorer, in sickness and in health, in joy and in sadness, as long as we both shall live." We had talked about those words so often.

But now, once again, there was no talking. Tracy's voice was silenced by the ventilator; and his hands—hands which had written me so many letters filled with anguish and love and humor—those hands were now too weak to hold a pen. He mouthed words sometimes, around the breathing tube: "I love you." And he could nod yes or no.

At first, when he seemed anxious to communicate, I encouraged him to think of one or two words that would help me know what he was thinking. I would say the alphabet aloud, slowly, until he nodded at a letter; I wrote that letter down and we started again, repeating the process until we finished a word or I figured it out.

"T...R...A...S...H... Oh, honey, don't worry. I put the trash out this week. I remembered."

"S...H...I... Oh! Do you need a bed pan?"

It worked, sort of, and could be funny. But it was very tedious and not very satisfying. After a few times, we stopped.

I did all the talking now. I told Tracy about the kids, the grandchildren, my work. I read the news aloud, told him about the Democratic National Convention, reported on the Olympics. I did crossword puzzles aloud, something we'd done together in many other hospital rooms. I read poetry, sang songs, recited the 23rd Psalm.

And I made signs. All through those weeks, I made a new sign every day, to hang where he could see it at the foot of his bed. When I was leaving for a few days, returning to Michigan to work briefly before rushing back to Columbus, I made signs for the nurses to post each morning I was gone. Using colored markers on a yellow lined pad, I wrote the date and a cheery greeting in big embellished block letters. I chose my few words carefully, leaving a different message each day:

"We love you!"

"Happy 4th Birthday, Sammy Jo!"

"Today is Sunday: a good day to get well!"

"See you tomorrow, honey!"

I wasn't certain he could see or read the signs, but I never stopped making them. And I never stopped talking to him, talking with him. Trying to will him well one more time.

I loved and cherished. Respected and encouraged. Helped any way I could think of, and asked others when my help was not enough. Not because we had spoken those vows, but because the vows were who we were and how we loved.

The words were important. Even if we could not talk about them.

A Leg to Stand On

I can picture this as if it were yesterday:

Tracy, tall and thin, skinny actually, leans back on the little silver-blue Nissan in our driveway, standing on one leg, the other bent up and resting against the car behind him. He crosses his arms loosely, casually, across his body. There's a slight tilt to his hip and the hint of a smile on his face; it gives my husband of two months a jaunty, rakish look.

I love this man, I think to myself.

And then, in the warm sun of a September afternoon, he looks at me and says, "I think I'll go for a drive."

Not an earth-shattering announcement. Except that a pair of crutches leans against the car, too, and his right leg, the one bent up and resting on the door, the one most of us use for the gas pedal and the brake—that leg ends just below the knee in a thick bandage. No calf, no ankle, no foot.

I am struck with panic. I'll come with you, I say.

"No, I'll go by myself." And he does.

He is back before long. He crutches to the front steps, where I sit waiting, breathing better now that he has returned.

"It's okay," he says, sitting down next to me. "I can drive with my left leg."

And that was that.

Amputation was one of Tracy's greatest fears—and had been for a long time, ever since a long-ago hospital stay in Ann Arbor, Michigan, not long after he was diagnosed with diabetes.

That hospitalization was supposed to be a training session, helping new patients learn to manage the disease. But diabetic management in the early 1960s was frighteningly inadequate by comparison with today; and hospitals back then still used a lot of group wards, rather than private rooms. Tracy shared the men's diabetic ward with patients of all ages—and at all stages of diabetic complication. During his time there, he watched a man die in the bed next to him. He also saw plenty of amputees, and at age 13 he concluded that might be worse than death.

Given enough time and opportunity, the high blood sugar that comes with diabetes will destroy nerves all through the body, but it starts with the tiniest nerve endings furthest from the heart, those at the ends of the extremities, most commonly the feet (but also, as Tracy learned later, the fingers). By his late 30s, Tracy had lost most of the feeling in his feet. He had told me this, and I observed that he had a slightly unusual gait, picking up and putting down his feet in a way that was just a little different. Still, except for the fact that tickling his toes produced no reaction, "I don't feel a lot in my feet" didn't mean much to me until the time, a year or so before we were married, when he spent one whole day annoyed at having misplaced his car keys. Changing his clothes after work, the keys fell out of one of his shoes.

After that, we both had more respect for *lack of feeling in the feet*.

From then on, Tracy was very conscientious about caring for his feet. He paid close attention to any irritation and was under a doctor's care for four months prior to our wedding trying to clear up a small blister on one heel. But a week in Maine—climbing the rocks at Pemaquid Point with his daughters a few days before the wedding, hiking up the uneven path to our cottage in Christmas

Cove, standing all through the ceremony in the Harrington Meeting House, and dancing the Tennessee Waltz (with me) and the Virginia Reel (with Michelle) at our reception—kicked that blister-wound into an intense infection.

Three days into our honeymoon wandering the Maine coast, Tracy and I returned to the Portland Jetport and rebooked our tickets home. Once in Toledo, I drove Tracy's big blue Chevy van for the first time and took him straight from the airport to the Toledo Hospital emergency room.

The next few weeks were, for me, a crash course in navigating through the medical system—and being the wife of a patient. Seven months earlier, when Tracy had been gifted with the kidney transplant, I was his significant other but not his wife; remarkably, even his mother and siblings expected, and accepted, that I would be the primary contact for the doctors during and after that surgery. But Tracy himself managed all the communication and decision-making prior to the transplant. And he wanted that surgery. More than anything. We both did.

This time, everything was different. We were doing everything possible to avoid surgery.

We'd been married less than a week when we arrived at the hospital, Tracy clearly sick with infection. The ER staff immediately found a bed for him, so he could lie down. In short order, the hospital admitted him. Then, for three weeks, assorted doctors fought the infection that was marching from his heel up his ankle.

Tracy was feverish all through that time, moving in and out of reality from day to day and hour to hour. "Are we going bowling today?" he asked one day as I arrived at his bedside. (Is this temporary, I wondered? I sure hoped so.)

Some days he was perfectly lucid and talked intelligently with the doctors; other days, he was in a fog of confusion and unreality. So I tried to be there to hear the doctors' reports, and learned to pester them by phone if I had missed their visits. I offended one doctor by asking a few too many questions: "Clearly, you have no confidence in me," he said, his voice curt even over the telephone. "Perhaps you should find someone else." Trying not to dissolve into tears, I asked if anyone in his family had ever been seriously ill in the hospital. I was a wife now; I was not backing down.

One day, I arrived at Tracy's room just as the nurses were changing the dressing on his foot. Several times now, the doctors had taken him to surgery to clean out the wound. "Debreeding," they called it. I was confused until I looked up the word and realized it was only pronounced de-breed; it was spelled "debride" and meant removing dead tissue. I knew they wanted the wound to heal from the inside out, and it was important to me to understand the terms. But the word did not prepare me for the reality of debridement. Tracy was alert and sharp the day I arrived during the dressing change, and he wanted me to know what we were dealing with. The nurse moved to the side so I could see.

I gazed at Tracy's ankle. But it didn't look like an ankle. It looked like an eight-inch-long triangle of raw meat. I could see the bone. I don't believe I said a thing; I hope I didn't gasp.

"I thought you should see it," Tracy said.

"Yes," I agreed.

I wondered how the small wound he had been soaking every morning before and after the wedding, up until we cut short our honeymoon, could have become so quickly this gigantic crater of raw flesh. And I wondered how his body could possibly heal "from the inside out," regenerating enough tissue to turn this crater back into an ankle.

But I did not say that.

"Yes," I said. "Now I can see what they're doing."

We continued to hope. I continued to ask the doctors every question I could think of.

Then one day, as I was about to bring Sarah and Michelle for a visit with Dad at Toledo Hospital, Tracy called, struggling—and then failing—to maintain his composure. "They want to cut off my leg," he choked out.

An hour or so later, the girls comfortably set up at home with a video, I arrived at the hospital to find him asleep on his back, clutching to his chest a photo of the two of us smiling at our wedding.

The decision was ours, ultimately: amputation while the infection had only reached the calf, allowing for a healthy stump below the knee to accept the holding-cup of a prosthesis; or continued fighting and hospitalization for perhaps a year, after which, if we were lucky—best case scenario—he would have a seriously compromised foot and leg. The chances for an active life were far better with a prosthetic leg than with a permanently malfunctioning "real" one, the surgeon advised. Tracy was a bird hunter, skeet shooter and avid outdoorsman. It was a hard decision, and a scary one, but he opted for the better odds.

Our one-month anniversary was a busy day in the O.R. There were several emergency surgeries, so Tracy's scheduled amputation got pushed back three or four times. I tried to be upbeat and take his mind off what lay ahead. When they finally rolled him away, after hours of waiting, tears seeped from the corners of his eyes, dripping onto the pillow on the gurney.

Late that night, I waited outside his room with his mother and his sister and brother, Cristal and Dexter. When the nurse finished her ministrations, she came out to report. Tracy was sleeping. We could go in one at a time, just for a minute.

"It only takes your breath away once," I thought afterward. "Just that first time you see one lump under the blanket that is shorter than the other. After that, you know what to expect and it's not so scary. It's just sad."

A few days later he came home with crutches and we embarked on married life.

There was much to come, for both of us, as he learned to live without his right leg: A long healing process made longer by one rogue stitch in the stump that hid from the doctor for several months. A few painful falls when his mind and body forgot there was no leg to stand on. Physical therapy to gain confidence going up and down stairs on crutches. Learning not to care too much when people glanced sideways after noticing his pant leg pinned up in mid-air. Then, months later, learning to balance on a prosthesis and trying to "feel" the ground, the steps, the accelerator and the brake pedal through that plastic and steel replacement for a leg.

But for Tracy, the most difficult challenge was not physical at all. It was much deeper, and more frightening: daring to trust that he was still a man, still needed, still a whole person to himself, to others, and most of all to me.

Tracy and I did not disagree often. We argued, of course; we didn't see eye to eye on everything. He was always irritated by my tendency to be late. I was easily annoyed by his ultra-competitive approach to skeet shooting. And we frequently took opposing political views. But we never fell into patterns of bickering or said deliberately hurtful things to each other.

A few months into our marriage, though, we had the only argument that ever reduced me to tears. It began with some insignificant concern, now long forgotten, but it came around to the fact that in my several days "away" each week, working at Ohio Wesleyan, I would sometimes meet groups of colleagues, male and female, for lunch or a drink after work or dinner. I had been a working woman for almost twenty years, and this was a long-ingrained habit. This was how I had met Tracy in the first place.

But, of course, Tracy was not part of these gatherings now. He was two hours north, at home in our house.

The parallels had not occurred to me before the night of our big fight; but to Tracy, these far-away social occasions looked dangerous and fraught with peril, especially when I mentioned the chemistry professor with the diabetic dog, or maybe it was the theater director, once too often.

His emotions tumbled out: Might I not find I preferred one of those college professors in Ohio? In fact, wasn't it likely? Indeed, why wouldn't I find someone else more appealing, some man who was more attractive, more...*whole?*

And there it was. The fear that hid itself in anger.

What he actually said was: "After all, I'm just a one-legged cripple."

My head exploded in silent horror. Not the horror he feared, of repugnance at his "incomplete" body, but something completely different and much worse. Horror that he could feel that way, that I might have said or done something to make him feel that way, that I hadn't known. And the biggest horror of all: that he could conceivably turn away from me because he thought me capable of turning away from him.

As painful as all of that was—for him to admit, for me to hear, for us to discuss—it was the beginning of a much deeper stage in our relationship. Once he could name the fear that threatened his self-confidence, I found words to express the joy I felt in our relationship; a joy that I had never known, not even a little, in my many years of single life before meeting him. No way was I going to find some other man more interesting or attractive. He was my choice. My white knight. My prince.

And while he only had one leg to stand on, he was all the man I wanted, and more.

But, yes, I could see now how he might have worried about that.

He didn't ask me to, but I stopped socializing so much with my male colleagues. Tracy was far more important to me than any lunch or cocktail hour.

Eventually, the amputation of Tracy's right leg came to seem almost insignificant, to both of us, except in the ways it added character to our lives. After he acquired a flesh-colored swim leg (no metal parts to rust in the water), he loved plunging into Crystal Lake on our family vacations, then later watching the startled faces of children as they walked past his chaise lounge on the beach and saw the water gushing out of a hole in the bottom of his "foot." When we and the girls settled into a hot tub at a resort in the Upper Peninsula, we all giggled uncontrollably when Tracy's foot popped up unexpectedly, over and over, in the center of tub; despite his best efforts, the hollow leg refused to stay underwater until it had time to fill.

Over time, as his stump reshaped itself, Tracy ended up with several prosthetic legs in the back of our closet. The legs provided endless entertainment for our toddler grandchildren who always found them and dragged them out to see if, maybe this time, they could manage to walk with one, just like Grampa.

A year after the amputation, Tracy went back to bird hunting, bushwhacking through the wild country on his prosthetic leg to the amazement of other hunters. I went along now and developed my own love of bird hunting. I never did any shooting, but I learned to walk just behind Tracy's shotgun, following Jess, our English setter. We became a team: Jess would go on point. Tracy would position himself to find firm, stable footing. And I would "walk up the bird," dropping to the ground when it flushed from hiding in a thunderous whirring of wings in flight. Often enough, Tracy's shot was good. Jess would bound out joyously to find and retrieve the pheasant or quail or woodcock. I would stand up and start to breathe again.

And some time later we would cook the bird at home.

"10/94—Very good. Used liver pate for the fois gras," I wrote beside a recipe for woodcock breasts with cognac.

"10/95—Great, but a little too much Tabasco for Tracy's taste," I noted next to the Dream Grouse recipe.

"1/1/98—Fantastic! Used heavy cream and pinot noir this time."

We even created an original crockpot recipe which we called Pheasant Elegante, with celery, onion, wine and green grapes.

We enjoyed every part of hunting.

Over time, Tracy's "good" foot became much more of a problem than the prosthetic leg. When he found his foot bloody after a day up north with his hunting buddies (I was busy at home this time, focusing on Christmas crafts), he knew that trip was over. "Yeah, I noticed you were sort of walking on the side of your foot," one of the other hunters said, as Tracy packed his bags for the unplanned drive home. "It didn't seem to bother you so I didn't say anything."

And that was how we happened to learn about "Charcot changes" in the foot and ankle, a degenerative bone disorder that is one more complication of diabetes. From then on, along with the prosthetic right leg, Tracy strapped a custom molded brace onto his left leg, to keep the heel, ankle and calf in alignment.

At the end of his life, many people who knew him had no idea and were surprised to learn that Tracy was an amputee. The loss of a leg, as frightening and unwelcome as it was when it happened, turned out to be just a small bump in the road. It did not stop him, or us, from much of anything.

But we didn't know that at first. On that sunny fall afternoon in 1990, when he went out for his first test drive alone, all we knew was that he could still get in the driver's seat and go somewhere, anywhere. And that was enough.

It was a beginning.

A few days later, we went out for a Sunday drive, exploring the countryside within easy reach of our still-new-to-us home. This time, we left the little Nissan at home and took the van. Tracy drove with the stump of his right leg resting on the wide console between the high front seats, his left foot on the pedals. Across from him in the passenger seat, I sat with our rambunctious new bird dog, the English setter puppy we called Jess, in my lap. Tracy was already training Jess to retrieve, sitting one-legged on the back porch with the puppy on a long check cord.

Tracy guided the van around an unfamiliar corner. In the autumn sun, the browning corn fields turned gold. There was country music on the radio and an open road in front of us.

I thought to myself, I've never been happier.

Give Us This Day

A year or two after we were married, Tracy and I began church shopping.

Sunday mornings, at least once every few weeks, we would choose a church—sometimes from the yellow pages, sometimes from the Saturday listings in the Toledo Blade's religion page, sometimes from our random drives around the area—and attend a service. Tracy wore a suit, or at least a jacket and tie; I dressed in a skirt and jacket or dress pants. We arrived in plenty of time; Tracy always wanted to be there early, maybe just so as not to draw attention with our entrance.

Afterward, we usually were quiet for the first few minutes of the drive home. Eventually, one or the other of us would offer a tentative comment or observation, not wanting to speak too firmly in case the other had a very different view. But that was a needless worry. Our gut reactions to the varied services and congregations were very similar.

Sometimes, our responses were embarrassingly superficial.

Tracy: That's not the one—I think people should dress up a little for church. And what's with standing up and talking about your day care business?

Jennifer: That sermon about the devil being behind every bush? That is definitely not the right place for me.

Tracy: We can't go there—we'd be the biggest donors in the church. Our old Jeep was the nicest car in the parking lot. They'd be after us to run everything.

Jennifer: I can't attend a church with an electric organ. I need really good music.

Tracy: A little too new age for me.

Jennifer: Not enough depth for me.

The first time we attended Epworth United Methodist Church, we both felt comfortable—with the sermon, the theology, the music, the balance between formality and friendliness. But it was a big church, bigger than either of us had ever attended and bigger than what we had in mind. We kept looking.

Every so often we returned to Epworth, and each time came away saying, "Too bad it's so big; otherwise it could be the right place."

After maybe a year of "shopping" and the third or fourth return visit, we received an invitation to a new-member information meeting at Epworth. We said yes and ended up joining the church on Epworth's 100th anniversary Sunday.

Tracy and I both grew up in the Congregational denomination. We each received an inscribed Bible in Sunday School, I at age 9, he at 12. Three decades later, we both brought those Bibles into our marriage, something we only discovered while organizing bookshelves in our new home.

As a child in Massachusetts, I and my family attended the First Church in Weymouth, a traditional white clapboard meetinghouse on a hill with a tall steeple and a long history. It really was the "first" church, founded in 1623, just three years after the Pilgrims sailed to Plymouth. The church claimed Revolutionary War leaders and signers of the Declaration of Independence among its "early" (only 150 years after its founding) members. Abigail Adams—wife of America's second president, John Adams, and mother of the sixth, John Quincy Adams—grew up in the church; her father was the minister there for forty-nine years.

In Michigan, where the state itself was 214 years younger than that New England church, Tracy's family attended the rural Madison Congregation. Services took place in a modest ranch house, renovated and remodeled into a suitable worship space by members of the congregation, including Vohne Church.

Tracy and I both had vivid memories of our childhood ministers.

The no-nonsense school bus driver, Miss Gorney, was Tracy's pastor throughout his childhood and a key mentor in his youth. (Many years later, she visited him in the hospital after his amputation, bringing with her the husband she had eventually married—who walked on a prosthetic leg. After all those years, she was still providing guidance and encouragement.)

I remembered my first Massachusetts minister mostly as a droning voice on Sunday mornings, and mostly in contrast to the next pastor, Rev. Schoonmaker. Since my father was on the pastoral search committee, I met this candidate across the dinner table at our house before hearing him from the pulpit; and was surprised to discover that his voice was the same in both settings. He seemed to be talking personally to me, whether in the dining room or the sanctuary. Suddenly, I found it easy to listen to the sermon.

When my family moved to New York, we left the picture-postcard New England church for a brand-new modern building, round with a sort of abstract teepee-style copper roof; the building fund ran out of money before buying pews so the seating was on temporary folding chairs. The folding chairs turned out to be so easily rearranged for different programs that the congregation ultimately abandoned the idea of permanent pews altogether. In this church, the pastor often quoted Shakespeare along with scripture; I was intrigued.

In our quite different churches and communities, Tracy and I both attended Sunday School and youth fellowship. I remained active a bit longer, finding through church a different set of high school friends, some memorable experiences including the annual youth fellowship ski trip, and a boyfriend.

By the time we met, though, neither of us had been connected with a church for well over a decade. I went to church with my parents whenever I was visiting and always enjoyed those Sunday services; but I had never been inspired to add church into my independent life. I wasn't sure what I really believed. Tracy had married and started a family at 18; he'd not been drawn to a congregation, either. But as we began our life together, we both felt the need, and the desire, for a deeper spiritual connection.

And so we went church shopping.

By now, the loss of his leg was past history for Tracy, but the experience continued to resonate with him. He didn't tell me about it for a long time; but one night after the amputation, while he was still in the hospital, Tracy had hit a low point.

"My mind spun out of control, redefining who I now was, a one-legged man with a stump, a cripple, an amputee," he recalled a few years later, writing about that dark night. "I was no longer me."

Sensing that Tracy was in distress, his elderly roommate asked how he was doing. Here's how Tracy described that late-night experience:

> I did not respond for a long time. My mind was a scramble and the effort to formulate thought and articulate words was almost beyond me.
>
> I finally said, "Not too good."
>
> He said, "Now you listen to me, son, because I've been there

and I know. You gotta give it to the man upstairs. You gotta let him do his job, because that's what he's there for."

He waited a while, then asked, "Do you understand?"

I said, 'Yes.'

And I did. I don't know exactly how I did it, because I didn't say anything out loud but inside myself, I directed my thoughts to "the man upstairs." I said the two words I had never been able to say before in my life. 'Help me.' There were no bells, no music, no thunder and no angels, nothing visible or audible in response; only the immediate and tangible lifting of all my troubles and burdens. It was literally as if a tremendous weight had been removed from my shoulders. I thought clearly for the first time, and I knew who I was and what I had to do, but most of all I knew I would be okay.

For Tracy, the end of the story turned out to be positive, as he went on to explain in the story he eventually titled *The Man Upstairs*:

I don't know what happened that night, and I'm not writing this now to influence anyone else in their beliefs. I only know that what happened to me that night was as real as any experience I have ever had, before or since.

I understand now there are things worse than death and things worse than being handicapped. It may well be that the most horrifying experience of all is to be totally and absolutely alone. I know I will never be totally alone again. In the end, I gained more than I lost.

Before long, we began to look for a church.

We did not become leaders at Epworth. I worked for a while on the communications committee, served on an *ad hoc* mission statement committee, and sometimes taught Sunday School for the 3- and 4-year-olds, taking occasional grandchildren with me when they came to spend a weekend. Once, Tracy spoke to a lunch group at the church about organ transplantation. Mostly, we just fulfilled our modest financial pledge and attended services somewhat regularly; though not infrequently we opted instead for sports or jobs or family time on Sunday morning.

But going to church was always a deeply satisfying way to start a Sunday. And even with our very casual approach, Epworth became a steady, quiet foundation for our life together. We still dressed up for church. Both of us shied away from the contemporary worship hour, preferring the traditional service and familiar music. We both got teary sometimes while singing the hymns: "How Great Thou Art" reminded me of my grandparents; "The Old Rugged Cross" reminded Tracy of his childhood church. We knelt at the rail for communion, discussed or debated the sermons on the drive home, and always chose the midnight candlelight service on Christmas Eve.

A few years later, when Tracy's health became more challenging, we gained a new appreciation of our church connection. Tracy was amazed, a little embarrassed, and very comforted (much to his own surprise) when one of our ministers stopped in to visit during one of his five post-pancreas-transplant hospitalizations in Columbus. This was, after all, about 140 miles south of our church in Toledo.

After that, one or the other of the pastors often stopped at whatever hospital Tracy was in at the time, to visit with us before surgery or during recovery. There was always a prayer together, usually asking grace and guidance for the doctors as well as the patient, but mostly I remember comforting conversation, often entirely unrelated to the circumstances at hand.

Once, after Tracy was rolled off for that day's procedure, a cardiac ablation, I and our minister had a discussion about the Old Testament, prompted by my asking why we rarely included Old Testament scripture in our services. I distinctly recalled both a New Testament lesson and one from the Old Testament in the worship services of my youth, and I missed that historical element. Was it a cultural change? Did few Protestant churches anymore include the older readings? Or was it just not part of the United Methodist tradition, I asked? The answer was amazingly simple: not enough time in the service, basically. But we talked at length—about the significance of the Old Testament in the Jewish faith, in literature, and as a precursor of things to come—and when he left, I felt calm and reassured, ready for the uncertain wait in the hospital and whatever came after.

That simple reality—the sense of calm and well-being that always seemed to accompany or flow from my connection with the church—formed the foundation of my faith. At its most basic, life was just...better...with God in it. And with the fellowship of the church.

Years earlier, before marriage, before Tracy, I had talked casually about religion with the president of the United Methodist college where I then worked. He was an ordained minister as well as a college CEO. I, the public relations director at the college, was not a member of any church then; I thought it would be disingenuous to join one, I told him, because I didn't have "that kind" of faith and would only be joining for the fellowship. His response startled me: "That's a good enough reason. That's why many people join. You don't need any more reason than that."

Two colleges later, I found myself writing a feature article on faith and Catholic identity for the magazine published by Siena Heights, the Catholic college where I now worked. Again, I was surprised to discover that faith was not always a matter of dogma or doctrine; sometimes it was just about making sense of experience, making peace with life. Faith is simply "how I see the world," said one Adrian Dominican Sister, a scholarly scientist. "And the world is dependent on God."

By this time, Tracy and I had joined our United Methodist church. Working for a Catholic college initially had given me pause. Walking into Sacred Heart Hall on my first day of work at Siena Heights, I had wondered: What will this be like? Will I be comfortable here? The answers came to me through the Adrian Dominican Sisters, founders and sponsors of the college.

The Adrian Dominicans are women of intellect and joy: unafraid to be unique, undaunted by obstacle, and unabashed about challenging any authority figure, male or female, whom they view as misguided. ("St. Paul doesn't say much to me," one Sister told me to my astonishment, when we were discussing gender equity.)

One morning, soon after I started at Siena, Sister Miriam Michael, an eminent chemist and cancer researcher in her eighties with whom I had already debated issues of language, politics and medicine, arrived at Sacred Heart Hall wearing a long gauzy skirt, an oversized t-shirt and a huge sun hat. In her arms, she carried a great big basket of giant zucchini to share with all who wanted them.

"What a glorious morning!" she announced brightly to anyone who would listen.

Wow, I thought, I can only hope to have that radiance and vitality when I am 80. I knew, then, that I was going to be comfortable at Siena Heights.

Indeed, I became very comfortable, not just with the people but with the soul of the place. I attended Mass during college celebrations, found mentors and close friends among the Sisters, team-taught several classes with a priest, even spoke to students occasionally on the role of faith in my own life.

I have never been tempted to change churches or denominations; but I enjoy many kinds of worship and I freely embrace what makes sense to me, wherever I find it. I still go to Mass on special occasions at Siena Heights. I attend my sister's Unitarian fellowship when I'm in Massachusetts, my mom's Congregational church when I'm in Maine, and Epworth United Methodist when I'm at home.

The man upstairs seems to speak in all those places.

The Best Medicine

She makes me laugh," my brother said many years ago when I asked him about the girlfriend who would become his wife. At the time, I had been living in the Midwest for several years, first as a graduate student at the University of Minnesota, now as a communications professional at Adrian College in Michigan. Sam was in Boston. After several years doing environmental education in rural New England, he was now working on a master's degree in elementary education. We'd not spent much time together in recent years, but we were very good friends.

I was always fond of my little brother. Growing up, I tried to shield and protect him from bigger boys in the neighborhood and, sometimes, from our impatient older sister, Becky: "Oh, just let him win," I pleaded with her, when I thought his five-year-old heart would break at the loss of whatever board game we were playing.

Later, when he was 15 and I, 20, Sam and I spent six weeks traveling together, youth-hosteling through Europe on our way to visit that same sister, then living in Afghanistan with her husband. Sam visited me at college in Vermont several times, was a periodic guest at my apartment in New York City in the years right after college, and later came to see me at the Haystack Mountain School of Crafts in Maine where I spent my graduate-school summers working on an island.

Sam was my buddy, my pal. We were close. But as happy as I was for his engagement, I couldn't help feeling just a little bit resentful of this yet-unmet fiancée.

Tell me about her, I must have asked.

"She makes me laugh."

No doubt he said more, but that's what stuck with me. And it seemed odd at the time. I didn't think of Sam needing encouragement to laugh. And yet, just what did that mean?

Years later, when I was well settled in my own marriage, I recalled that comment, and smiled. Tracy made me laugh, too. What a gift it was! And yes, wasn't it just what I thought of when I considered why we were happy? In a life dependent on medical miracles, when every day included dozens of pills, multiple prescriptions, and checking the calendar for doctor appointments, laughter was very good medicine.

Tracy and I laughed in hospital rooms, he hooked up to IVs with me curled next to him on the bed. We laughed over strange news stories and stray kittens, bizarre dreams and the misadventures of our youth. We laughed over coffee before pre-dawn drives to dialysis. We laughed late at night when the house was cold and the bed warm. We laughed on Christmas morning, pulling silly surprises out of the stockings we filled for each other; and on New Year's Eve, cooking elaborate wild game dinners that we served each other on our best china; and on vacation with the family, watching wide-eyed toddlers make sense of the bare foot of a prosthetic leg standing alone in a corner.

Sometimes I heard Tracy laughing alone. The first time that happened, I came to inquire: he was watching television by himself and laughed out loud at something funny. Had I ever done that, I wondered? I think of him now, any time something makes me laugh unexpectedly, with no one else around to hear. I wonder if he is smiling at those moments.

For Tracy, making a funny comment or a wry observation could be a defense mechanism or an ice breaker in an awkward social situation; but most of the time, it was just a natural way to navigate through life.

At a family party a month before our wedding, I sat at a table outdoors with Tracy and his siblings, Dexter and Cristal, and experienced for the first time the over-the-top laughfest that happened each time those three came together. Their non-stop sparring and rapid-fire humor left me breathless with laughter. And wondering how I would ever keep up.

Looking back, I wonder if Tracy's sister ever felt threatened by me, as I had been by Eve.

"She makes me laugh," Sam had said.

Did I make Tracy laugh? I don't know; maybe he just helped me. But we sure laughed together, day after day—sometimes a chuckle, sometimes a guffaw, sometimes unbridled hilarity. It was good medicine for love and marriage, and also for building our new family.

Vacationing for the first time with our two younger daughters, Tracy and I sat down one evening to play cards with Sarah and Shelly. We had driven all day to reach Michigan's Upper Peninsula where, some weeks ago, we had rented a cabin sight unseen. Now seen, it was clear the delights of the place had been dramatically oversold; but it was late, and a solution would have to wait until morning.

"Let's play cards."

With wildflower weeds in a juice glass for ambiance, we gathered around the formica-topped kitchen table for a game of euchre. I didn't know the game, but playing cards was a part of life for Tracy and for the girls, whose earliest memories included hours of shuffling practice with Dad.

"Don't worry," 14-year-old Sarah reassured me. "This is an easy game."

"You'll get it right away," 11-year-old Michelle chimed in, encouragingly.

If the girls can do this, I reasoned silently, surely I can, too. After all, I have two college degrees. How hard can it be?

Ah, but cards were not a big part of my life up to then. I watched in amazement as Tracy and the girls magically kept track of cards played and cards to come, strategies to capture the good ones and tactics to avoid the undesirables.

And how can anyone remember the ins and outs of that bower thing? I wondered.

I was game to try, but my efforts were, well, comical. Before long I was engulfed in waves of unstoppable laughter. When I dissolved into convulsive snorting, that was it. The girls hooted, the laughter contagious, and soon all four of us were gasping for breath.

My new family had bonded! Laughter was good medicine.

Humor became a genuine survival strategy for Tracy and me. Even in dire circumstances, a good laugh put the situation in a better light and reminded us that, no matter what else might be threatened, our relationship was solid.

In the weeks just after our wedding, as doctors wrestled with the infection in his foot and he wrestled with a pain beyond the reach of painkillers, Tracy (on his good days) lightened our conversation with his quirky reflections on the medical experts—nurses, specialists, researchers—who trooped in and out of his hospital room many times a day. Each one in succession invariably asked the same deep and probing questions: his name, date of birth, condition, medical history, what prescriptions he was taking.

Tracy quickly dubbed the scholarly pathologist in the bunch

"Bug Man." We fervently hoped this nerdy, awkward physician—who seemed more comfortable with bacteria than with live bodies—would indeed identify all of the "bugs" invading Tracy's wound and the antidotes that would kill them off. As serious as the battle was, though, we found relief in humorous analysis of his daily visits, his comical head-down rushing through the hallways, and the stereotypical way he pushed his glasses up onto the bridge of his nose several times during each brief report. In the end, Bug Man's efforts were in vain; but we appreciated his knowledge and diligence as much as the opportunities he gave us to laugh. It was self-medication of the best sort.

In the years that followed, at the kissing corner in every hospital—that turn in the corridor where we would say goodbye before he rolled off to his next operation and I headed to the gift shop, the cafeteria, the waiting room—Tracy invariably made a lighthearted comment that made even the hospital aides chuckle. As I went off to think, or not think, to hope, to pass a few hours, I would be left with the image of him on the gurney, smiling his crooked smile, winking intimately, and lifting his hand in a cheery wave as he disappeared through the do-not-enter double doors.

A crooked smile. Laughter. Good medicine. He made it through all those surgeries.

Sunday, June 20, was beautiful day in Michigan in 2004.

For Tracy and me, it was a day of mixed emotions. We, and our family and friends, most especially our daughter Michelle (who had long since abandoned her nickname, Shelly), were nervous and excited about the week to come. On Tuesday morning, Tracy and Michelle were scheduled for side-by-side surgeries at OSU; the doctors would remove one of Michelle's healthy kidneys and put it to work in Tracy's body. His first kidney had lasted twelve years.

Now, after thirty months of dialysis and declining health, Tracy had ventured a guess, or a prayer, that Michelle's kidney could turn things around: "I might get ten more years," he'd said.

We were anxious but hopeful as we prepared to drive to Columbus, spend Sunday night in a hotel, then check into the Medical Center first thing in the morning for a long day of pre-operative tests and double-checks. Michelle would drive down with a friend on Monday for her afternoon check-in.

As we packed for the trip, though, our house was quieter than usual. Someone was missing. The day before, on an equally beautiful Saturday morning, the two of us and our faithful four-legged companion—the handsome Birdfinder J'espere, our Jess— had driven to the veterinarian's office. There, beneath a beautiful oak tree, I sat on a blanket on the ground and Jess hobbled over to collapse into my lap. From his puppy days in the front seat of our old van, Jess had always claimed my lap, even as he grew well beyond lap-dog dimensions. On this gentle morning, Tracy sat beside me on a folding chair, leaning over, and together we stroked the silky coat of our loyal friend one last time. Deaf, emaciated and riddled with cancer, unable to get into the car on his own or even keep his footing on the smooth surface of the vet's newly paved parking lot, Jess raised his liquid brown eyes once more in adoration, then lay back still. We cried until the tears stopped. Then Tracy and I drove home, silent and empty.

Now, as we folded Tracy's bathrobe into a suitcase and checked toothbrushes and medications for the stay in Columbus, we talked quietly about all that Jess had brought into our life: what a great hunting dog he was, and what a wonderful family dog, too, never complaining when the grandchildren petted his eyes or pulled his tail, always wanting to be with us—except when he chose to run off and explore the neighborhood. How a hunting friend had sent him to us as a puppy right after we were married, when Tracy had just lost his leg, and how, remarkably, that had turned out to be just the right thing at just the right time. And how, today, we missed the sound of his toenails clicking on the kitchen floor, and the thump of his wagging tail whenever we came near.

We packed the car, backed out of the driveway, and headed for the highway south as the sun angled toward the horizon. I was at the wheel; driving was hard for Tracy now, because of the pain in his fingers. We were silent for a while, lost in thoughts of the past and questions about the future.

Then, after a while, Tracy said, "What do you think all these people are doing?"

Every few miles, we passed groups of men, women and children gathered in apparent party mode on the grass facing the interstate. They lounged in lawn chairs, leaned back on tailgates, parked themselves on the hoods of cars and trucks. They appeared to be laughing in good spirits.

What was going on? We speculated on the possibilities, happy for the distraction. An eclipse perhaps? No, we would have been aware of that. Some annual bird migration? What about the buzzards that return to Ohio every year? No, Tracy said, that happens earlier. What about all those birds that come north and fly over Lake Erie every year? Look and see—do those people have binoculars? I was fixated on the bird idea.

Traffic was heavy that day, and colorful, too: I looked left as yet another semi-tractor trailer inched past me, and admired the artwork on its box: a flashy racecar emblazoned with names in fiery lettering.

"That's it!" Tracy said suddenly. "The races. They're all going home."

I was still in the dark.

This was a Nascar race weekend at the Michigan International Speedway, he reminded me. I nodded. We both knew that; our daughter Cindy and her husband worked long hours in security at the track during every race weekend. The races were over now and the teams were heading south, Tracy said. The colorfully decorated semis were carrying the race cars, though not the drivers, back to their home bases in Columbus, Nashville and other cities further south.

"That's what's going on," Tracy said, gesturing to the field we were passing, where yet another group of merrymakers was camped on lawn chairs. "They're not waiting for an eclipse or a bird migration or the sunset. They're Nascar fans waiting to see the trailers go by."

"No!" I burst out in complete disbelief. "That can't be true!" But I whipped my head around to glance past Tracy's profile toward the field by the highway. Young men and old women and teenagers and kids were jumping and cheering and waving down the road at the flashy semi that had just passed us.

It was true.

"I can't believe it!" I said giggling. "This is the dumbest thing I've ever seen. Who would waste a perfectly good Sunday evening sitting on the side of a superhighway to watch a semi drive by at seventy miles an hour? It's gone in two seconds. And who cares anyhow?"

Plenty of people, apparently.

We laughed and laughed. A few miles further on, we exited from the Interstate and continued toward Columbus on U.S. 23. The groups grew smaller and further apart. A while later, we pulled off the road for a fast-food supper at Wendy's. By now it was dark; but even here, bystanders were milling in the parking lot next to the road, still watching the traffic. Tracy and I were eating at a table inside, when a tank-topped woman burst in the door, eyes wide, calling to another table, "It was Bobby Labonte! You missed it!"

Tracy and I looked at each other and giggled into our hamburgers.

It takes all kinds, we agreed, settling back into the car for the last leg of the drive to our hotel in Columbus. We chuckled most of the way, talking about who we were, who they were, and the different ways we all found fun and satisfaction and humor in life. Good medicine.

We were ready for whatever the next day would bring.

Humor was Tracy's way of stilling his own fears. And mine. He tried hard not to worry me and felt bad about burdening me with his medical challenges, though I never felt them as burdens. He made me laugh every day.

Back in 1990, fourteen years before our Nascar revelation, when we were newlyweds of one month, Tracy called me at home from his hospital bed in Toledo, the morning after the amputation. He called me! He was the patient—the guy who had just had his leg cut off below the knee, who had just experienced the thing he had feared the most since becoming diabetic at age 13. I was supposed to be calling him.

But the phone rang before 8:30 in the morning. I had just gotten up after that late and draining night. The phone rang and it was Tracy calling. Just to make sure I was okay.

To make sure *I* was okay?

His voice was cheery and bright, pain-free for the first time in weeks, and ringing with the possibility of laughter.

"That was some night," he said. "Are you okay?"

I love this man, I thought, not for the first or the hundredth time.

"I'm okay," I said. "How 'bout you?"

And then we both laughed. The medicine began its healing work.

So Much to Live For

July 11, 2004. Sunday. Four days after our fourteenth wedding anniversary.

Tracy was sick. Sicker, perhaps, than he had ever been.

The doctor had made sure I understood that the night before, at the end of an exhaustive day of testing and evaluation. After seeing Tracy through dozens of complicated medical crises over the years and watching him recover again and again, the doctor announced this latest diagnosis with more gravity than I'd ever heard in his voice. He ushered me out of the hospital room, into the hallway beyond Tracy's hearing.

"It is pneumonia," he said. "He is very sick."

He paused, stepped back, then spoke again. "This will be a long fight. We can only hope his heart is strong enough for it."

Pneumonia.

On the surface of it, pneumonia seemed simpler, less serious, less of a big deal than many prior diagnoses. After all, we'd been through multiple organ transplants, a couple of heart attacks, and a bunch of medical situations with more exotic names than this. I knew lots of people who'd had pneumonia. Some didn't even go to the hospital.

And yet...

"He is very sick. We can only hope..."

Looking back, I think Tracy knew, before anyone else, that he was in really bad shape. And that it was more than just a difficult recovery from his second kidney transplant.

He knew on Wednesday when he accepted the wheelchair I rented to take him to several doctor appointments. He knew on Thursday, when he struggled mightily for the breath to describe his symptoms, slowly and articulately, at one of those appointments. He knew Friday morning, slumped at our kitchen table, when he said, "I think I need to be in the hospital."

Never before had he accepted the indignity of a wheelchair ("I will walk") or volunteered to enter the hospital, especially on a Friday: "Nothing happens in a hospital over the weekend," he always said, speaking from experience. "Let's take care of it at home."

But he must have known: this time was different. Over the phone, his doctor agreed; he knew his patient well: "If Tracy says he belongs in the hospital, he needs to be in the hospital," he said when I called. "Get him to the emergency room."

Sitting in the lift chair we had bought in a hurry (something else he agreed to, after he was unable to get up from the couch), Tracy was calm but clear when he said, "You'd better call an ambulance."

"I'll drive," I insisted. And again, "I can drive you."

I always drove him to the hospital in emergencies. We would talk together on the way and my miracle man would gear up for the boredom and debilitation that always came with a hospital stay. For every day in the hospital, you need at least a week to recuperate, he claimed.

"Let me drive you," I pleaded again. "We'll get there faster."

But Tracy knew that this time was different. He was different.

"I don't think I can make it to the car," he said gently. "Just call."

A while later, I stood outside, weeping as I waved the ambulance into our driveway. Tracy had never before been so sick that I couldn't take him where he needed to go.

The hospital "weekend" that followed was different, too. This time, everything happened. Specialists with grave expressions trooped in and out, ordering tests and reading charts. One doctor, meeting Tracy for the first time, studied his history in silence and then said with some amazement, "Wow. And you're still here." Tracy and I laughed about that after he left.

Now it was Sunday evening. The Toledo doctors had determined Tracy was sick enough to jeopardize the vigorous kidney Michelle had given him three weeks earlier. He should be transferred from Toledo Hospital back to Columbus, they said; back to the care of his transplant team at the Ohio State University Medical Center.

Earlier in the day, Tracy's temperature had spiked high enough that the Intensive Care Unit nurses packed his body with ice. This was a new one on me: In the high-tech ICU jungle of whirring machines, beeping monitors, and blinking gizmos of all kinds, it was simple bags of ice, or their equivalent, that would bring his temperature down? But it worked.

After our daughters left the hospital late in the afternoon, Tracy snoozed for a while, exhausted by the day's events, as we waited to find out how and when he would be transported the 143 miles to Columbus. "You're the only one I can sleep with," he said gratefully, eyelids drooping, while I sat next to the bed, working a crossword puzzle.

"Yes, and you better keep it that way," I retorted, grinning. He smiled and dozed off.

Now, awake again, Tracy was in a reflective mood.

"I have so much to live for," he said, gazing intently at the pictures of our grandchildren taped to his TV monitor: Alexandra, Johnny and Sammy Jo at the zoo. Kayla smiling up from a picture book. DJ playing with his transformer men. Morgan pushing the doll carriage we had given her for her second birthday just a month ago. A seventh grandchild, a baby brother for Kayla, was due in a couple months.

"So much to live for," he said again, turning his eyes toward me. "I just need to fight this thing and get well again."

Demonstrating once again the determination and resilience that had made him the ultimate come-back kid, he was now cool (literally), calm and collected. He hardly seemed sick at all.

I gazed across the ICU at several other cubicles, each as wired and plugged-in as this one, dimly lit by the eerie glow of multiple LED diagnostic systems. The patients over there were really sick, I thought. Not like Tracy. He was seriously ill, sure; "very sick," the doctor had said. But look: He was already getting better, just like always.

"It would be too bad to die in a place like this," I reflected aloud.

This many years later, it sounds like an awful thing to have said, but I wasn't commenting on Tracy's condition. It was just an observation. And he took no offense. The place just seemed so stark and antiseptic.

It *would* be too bad to die in a place like that.

"Mmm," Tracy agreed, thoughtfully. "But you don't always have a choice."

That was not the response I had expected. It left me speechless.

That was the only time we mentioned the possibility of death. Oh, Tracy had alluded to dying in the past, but never seriously. Never in a way that demanded thought.

"Just make sure the next guy you marry is healthy," he had said one day, when he was frustrated with the demands of doctors' appointments on his schedule and mine. I dismissed that comment with a don't-be-ridiculous roll of my eyes.

Another time, after meeting with his financial advisor, he leaned against the kitchen counter in jeans and a down vest, explaining the value of a new "death benefit" feature in an IRA. "This will be good for you," he said, pointing his finger at me, trying unsuccessfully to interest me in the topic. I couldn't engage in the benefits of death.

Then there was the day I wrote his obituary prematurely, frightened by a call from another ICU nurse after Tracy's first heart attack: "You need to come," she had called my office to say. I drove to the hospital in a panic, simultaneously praying ("Not now, not yet, please God.") and composing an appropriate summary of his life in my head, as I challenged the speed limit to Toledo. During spells in the waiting room that day, I scribbled in a small notebook.

But my highway prayers were answered that time. Determination and resilience won. At the kitchen table, a few days later, I shared my notes with him.

"Not many people get the chance to rewrite their own obituary," I said with a grin.

He laughed, then made some key corrections and additions to my draft. We even discussed where "eventually" he would want to be buried and where the funeral should be.

But writing your obituary has nothing to do, really, with dying. Nor does planning the details of a funeral or burial, though I was grateful to know what he wanted when the time came. Those are after-death details.

Of dying itself—when and under what circumstances to give up the fight for life, what would be the minimum that made life worthwhile, what conditions would make giving up a better choice—we never spoke.

No doubt we should have had that conversation; and we surely would have done it later that last summer if we'd been able, but by then Tracy had no voice, silenced first by a breathing tube, later by a tracheostomy.

Part way through that summer of 2004, on a day when I was working in Michigan and our oldest daughter Cindy was "on duty" in Columbus, Cindy asked Tracy if he wanted to keep fighting.

He had the ventilator tube down his throat, an NG tube in his nose, an IV tube in his arm, a few other tubes for assorted bodily functions. A patchwork of white adhesive tape held it all in place on his body. All around him, monitors and machines whirred and beeped and blinked.

The tubes on Tracy's face were scheduled to be removed the next day—not because he was getting better, but because there is a limit to how long you can safely maintain those potential germ-highways into the body. I was excited about this change, though. I couldn't wait to kiss his tube-free face again, germs be damned. Tomorrow, the doctors would do a tracheostomy, sending oxygen to his lungs through a hole in his throat instead of through the breathing tube, and replace the nasogastric tube in his nose with a feeding tube directly into the stomach. Of course, there would still be no talking, because after the "trach" no air would cross the vocal cords, but I tried not to think about that. There would be other options for vocalizing in the future; we would deal with that later.

I characterized all the tubes—those in place and those to come—as "therapy," necessary treatments for his recovery. But Cindy had a public-safety officer's clear-eyed objectivity. She saw it as "life support." And she wanted to know what her father thought.

"Dad, do you want to be on life support?" she asked him directly. He nodded vigorously. (He could still nod vigorously at that point.)

"Do you understand what I'm talking about, Dad?" she persisted. She even wrote it down, in case he had trouble hearing. He nodded again. This time, his movement and his eyes betrayed annoyance and disgust: *Of course I know what you're talking about.*

Cindy laughed when she called me that night to tell me about it. "So Dad's in the hospital and I'm supposed to be taking care of him and instead we have a fight!"

But she could see that he was up for the fight. And it really wasn't a fight with her.

I'm not dying, he seemed to say. Can't you see? This is what I have to do to get better.

So we did not talk about death, even as death hovered all around. We shooed death away. And we—I, our daughters, family, friends—talked to Tracy about everything but death. The Detroit Tigers. Sarah's pregnancy. Sammy Jo's birthday. Michelle's recovery from the kidney donation. The weather. The news unless it was too depressing.

I read aloud to him: poetry, short stories, the 23rd Psalm. I sang to him, '60s folks tunes and old camp songs, "Kum Ba Yah" and "Tell Me Why." I did the daily crossword puzzle out loud, encouraging Tracy to send me the answers through ESP.

We talked about life.

And now, I kissed him. On my first visit after the removal of the breathing tube, as I leaned down, he reached up, cupped his hand around my head, and pulled me into his kiss with surprising strength. That was a good day! I was sure he was getting better.

But every positive development seemed to lead quickly to some new and darker complication.

On the good days, Tracy nodded or smiled or winked. Other days, he slept. On bad days, we didn't know if it was sleep, unconsciousness or some sort of coma. But he was fighting.

One day, young Dr. Barrett (they all seemed young) stopped by on his rounds. Tracy was not awake. The doctor checked vital signs, checked various electronic readings, checked the ever-thicker medical notebook chronicling the patient's ups and downs. Just as he was leaving, Tracy opened his eyes.

"Oh, honey, you're awake! Oh. Oh, wait. The doctor was just here—wait!"

I brought Dr. Barrett back and introduced him. Tracy looked straight at the doctor, nodded slightly, and lifted his hand a tiny bit from the bed. (He was weaker now.) The doctor took his hand and offered a greeting, man-to-man. "Hang in there," he said.

And then, turning to me: "This is good."

He could see. Tracy was still fighting.

Another day sometime later, the physical therapy team arrived while I was visiting. I teased Tracy about having not one but two personal trainers. Positioned on both sides of the bed, they gently lifted one leg at a time at the knee, working the calf (or the stump) slowly back and forth. Then they worked his arms in mock curls, bending them at the elbow, moving Tracy's wrists from the bed... to his shoulder...and back, slowly and gently. "Try to help," they encouraged him. I stood at the foot of the bed, watching.

After a few repetitions, the therapists settled his arms back on the blankets, then talked quietly and professionally across the bed, summarizing their observations for Tracy's case record. Suddenly, I pointed with excitement, alerting them: "He's doing it himself!"

Tracy's face strained with exertion as he struggled to lift his forearms from the bed. Slowly, exhaustingly, he succeeded. It was a far cry from the curls he had done at home with big hand weights, lying back on our coffee table as if it were an exercise bench—and a far greater victory. The therapists smiled. I clapped and cried.

Tracy had shown me he was not giving up. He was still in the fight.

But he had also shown me what kind of war it was.

In bed that night, my arms at my sides, I gazed at the hotel room ceiling and felt my hands. I wiggled my fingers, made fists, splayed my hands then lifted them effortlessly from the blanket, making right angles of my arms. I waved at the ceiling then reached high, stretching toward the roof, the stars, heaven.

How sick are you, when you can barely lift your hands off the bed? I wondered. What does it feel like to be so weak?

And what does it mean?

I couldn't go there.

I focused on the fighting.

Tracy and I certainly had many opportunities through the years to think about end-of-life issues. Before every surgical procedure, doctors and nurses asked if Tracy had a living will or any medical directives. We took the paperwork home each time, promising to take care of it; but at home we focused on living, making each day a good one and looking ahead. Did we think it bad luck to dwell on the possibility of a negative outcome? Maybe. I don't know. In any case, we never got around to discussing what efforts we would, or would not, want taken to sustain life if...if...if things did not go the way we hoped. The way we intended. The way we wanted.

So each time he was admitted—for the first kidney transplant, the leg amputation, the pancreas transplant, open heart surgery, finger amputations, and numerous other minor and major procedures— when hospital personnel asked, we admitted that, no, we had no living will, no advanced medical directives, no contingency plans. We had one plan and it was simple: the doctors would do the best they could, so Tracy could get on with life as well as he could.

Time and again, as he was about to be wheeled away for surgery, Tracy smiled and wished me well: "If I don't make it," he always said, "you will be the one who suffers." It won't be hard for me, he speculated; it's those left behind who will hurt.

But, neither of us ever expected him to die.

In June of 2004, when Tracy was admitted for the scheduled second kidney transplant, this one to be donated not by an accident victim but by his healthy daughter Michelle, we did intend to take care of the paperwork. We knew he was not in good shape; he was weaker and less healthy than he had ever been going into major surgery. Forty-three years of diabetes and the past two-and-a-half years back on dialysis had taken their toll. He took a big handful of pills each morning and again in the evening. His heart was weak and irregular, and had twice been jolted into action by the defibrillator implanted in his right shoulder. He had undergone cardiac ablation just two weeks earlier. He also had lost three fingers to amputation, each one painfully blackened and shriveled by progressive nerve death; and now, tiny signs of that evil decay had appeared on the ends of two more fingers.

So, yes, we agreed. We definitely should take care of that paperwork this time.

There was a long day of hurry-up-and-wait at the OSU Medical Center, as doctors and nurses prepared both Tracy and Michelle for the next morning's transplant surgery. We carried the paperwork around. I read it all while he was in various stages of pre-op.

And then, in a remarkable case of kidney transplant déjà vu, the surgical team stopped. "Wait," they said. "Not so fast." The risks might be too great, they said.

Back in 1989, when Tracy was already prepped and hooked up with an IV for his first kidney transplant, another surgeon had stepped back, worried about a cold sore on Tracy's lip that could, he pointed out, send herpes virus down the breathing tube into his body during surgery. Everything stopped, including my own breathing. The room turned red before my eyes and I leaned onto the gurney to keep from collapsing.

But Tracy, bare-chested under a sheet, and propped up on pillows, took a deep breath and made the best sales pitch of his career: He was ready, he said, in a voice measured and steady. The kidney was a match. And after a year on dialysis he had begun to go downhill. His health was not going to get any better than it was right then. He understood the risks and he was willing to take them, he said.

He paused; then offered his closing statement.

"I just think the patient should have some say."

Ultimately, his medical team agreed—and off he went.

Fifteen years later, the details were different but the overall picture much the same. There were significant risks, we all agreed. But Tracy's health, compromised as it was, would not improve without a new kidney. And we had our donor, right here, right now. The doctors laid out the pros and cons, and said it was our decision. They left the room, giving us a few minutes to think about it.

Neither of us said anything at first. Then Tracy asked me, "What do you think?"

"I don't know," I admitted slowly. "I can't quite see us turning around and going home. But...it's your decision..."

Another long pause.

"I just think I have to try," he said, finally. "I would always wish I had tried."

The medical machinery went back into action. The doctors gave Tracy something to counter the excruciating nerve pain in his fingers while he waited for one last round of evening dialysis before the early morning transplant.

Finally, I brought out that pesky paperwork.

But wait. The pain medication was out of whack. These doctors didn't know Tracy as well as his day-to-day medical team back home, and they'd given him too much of whatever it was. Tracy was loopy.

With two nurses as witnesses, he managed to sign his name to the paper giving me medical power of attorney. I knew he would want me to make decisions for him if he couldn't do it himself. But all those other detailed questions? What sorts of measures he would want taken to keep him alive under what kinds of circumstances? No way could he discuss those things in this incoherent state; and I truly did not know how he would answer such questions. We settled for the medical power of attorney.

By the next morning, he was lucid and clear-eyed, but there was no time. I got to the hospital before six and kissed him off to the operating room. The transplant went well. Michelle's vigorous 24-year-old kidney began working on the operating table. No three weeks of waiting this time around! Tracy was back in the business of peeing. And living.

The rest of the paperwork was forgotten, as it had been so many times before.

Things might have been very different if we had addressed those questions before the transplant. Maybe Tracy would have said, "Don't revive me if my heart stops." I don't know.

I do know that three weeks later, when he was "very sick" with pneumonia on his second day back at OSU, his heart did stop, while the doctors were at his bedside for morning rounds.

I had arrived in Columbus the night before, just one day after saying goodbye to my "already getting better" husband in Toledo, and found him in terrible shape. He had gone downhill incredibly fast. He wore an oxygen mask and had no breath to speak, even to me. It was all he could do to inhale and exhale. I was shaken to the core.

The next morning, they would not let me in to see him right away. I waited, wondered, worried. When finally I was allowed in, he had a breathing tube in his throat and fear in his eyes. Only later did I learn he had suffered cardiac arrest.

If, three weeks earlier, we had signed a DNR order ("do not resuscitate"), he probably would have died that morning. But we hadn't. The doctors were right there when he "coded" (as they say on TV, referring to "Code Blue") and they did whatever it took to restart his heart.

So now there was fear in his eyes, but there was also fight. He was not giving up.

On a warm Friday afternoon in late August, a month and half after that "Code Blue" incident, Dr. Denny called me at work.

I had come back to Michigan to spend a few days in the office. Tracy's sister Cristal had stayed at the hospital in Columbus; returning home Thursday night, she had reported, "Tracy was awake today! He gave me a big smile when I got to the room. He even smiled when I told him a funny story about Dexter giving me fits!" (They liked to joke about their brother, fondly known as Saint Dexter.) That was encouraging news. Maybe the beginning of getting better? I was even more excited than usual about heading back to Columbus after work that Friday.

The phone rang.

"Alumni Office. This is Jennifer."

"Jennifer Church? This is Dr. Denny."

There were four main doctors managing Tracy's case, two surgeons and two residents. Dr. Denny, the senior resident, spoke most often with me. A big jovial man, whose wife had recently given birth to their first child, he had been encouraging all summer long. Each time I asked in desperation, "But can he get well?" Dr. Denny said yes, though maybe he was less emphatic as the summer wore on. But he was impressed with Tracy's indomitable will to fight, to live.

Today's report, though, was more sober.

"We did another bronchoscopy today," he said, "to look more closely at the lungs. We're still studying the results. We believe the pneumonia is now either hemoraghic or necrotic."

What does that mean, I asked? And which is worse?

"Neither is good."

So, what are you telling me, I asked?

"I think he will either get very sick in the next few days—or he will overcome this like he's overcome everything else." It was important that I come back to the hospital. "But take your time," he cautioned. "Be safe. Don't break any speed limits."

I wondered briefly how someone who was sick enough to be in intensive care for more than six weeks could now "get very sick." Hadn't he been very sick from the beginning? How much more sick could he get?

Later I would realize that the conversation by telephone with Dr. Denny was the last time I had any contact with the medical team who had been my hospital "family" all summer long in the Surgical Intensive Care Unit. By the time I arrived at the OSU Medical Center that Friday night, Tracy had been moved from SICU to the Medical Intensive Care Unit. I didn't immediately comprehend the difference, but Tracy's condition was no longer considered a complication of, or even related to, the kidney transplant surgery.

I came to think of MICU as the place where patients went to die. Not all patients died, of course. But mine did.

That night, when I located the MICU and finally was allowed in, Tracy was sleeping calmly. He looked more peaceful than he had for weeks.

The nurse on duty was blunt. "If it's necrotic pneumonia, the prognosis is bad," she said quietly. "There's nothing they can do." She seemed too young to be so serious.

"Would that be the beginning...of the end of the road?" I asked.

"Yes," she said. "And it could be a short road." She wanted to make sure I understood.

Alright, I reasoned after the nurse left, this might be the beginning of the end. But, then again, it might not. They're "still studying" it. That's what Dr. Denny had said.

Alone with Tracy, I held onto the bed railing and talked to his sleeping body, gazing at his serene face.

"Hi, honey. It's me. I'm back, just like I promised." I paused.

"You're in a new room now." (It really was just a curtained cubicle. There appeared to be no real rooms in MICU.)

"And you're on a different floor." (I wondered if he was awake when they moved him, or if he even knew.)

What could he hear, lying there? Was he asleep? Was he unconscious? I hoped he could hear me. There were things I needed to say. I began speaking slowly.

"Tracy? Honey? The doctors say you're really sick now. They say it's really bad...and you might not get well." I paused again, forcing myself to think.

"You know how much I love you. And how much I want you to come home and come back to our life together. You've been fighting really hard for a long time. And...and I want you to fight; I've been encouraging you to fight all along.

"But..." I stopped and took a breath before continuing. "But if you're tired of fighting...if you think the fight is over and you don't want to do it anymore...it's okay."

In secret moments all summer, I had worried: How would we know if he didn't want to keep fighting? What if he was ready to let go? What if we were torturing him, just to keep him with us?

I wiped my eyes and spoke again.

"If you're too tired...and you're ready to go be with your mom... that's okay. I don't want to lose you; you know that. But if it's time…if you're ready…you can go. We'll be okay. I mean, we won't be okay. At first—we'll be terrible! But don't worry. Don't worry about the girls and the grandchildren. I'll take care of them. I can't be you—and they're going to want you—but I'll be there. I promise. Oh, God. Tracy, I love you so much."

And then, in a moment I will always treasure as a miracle, Tracy opened his blue eyes, looked right at me, and smiled. A beautiful knowing smile.

"Oh, honey!" I sniffled in my excitement. "Oh, Tracy, I'm so glad to see you!"

I knew from experience that this awakeness and with-it-ness might not last long, so I wiped my face and held his hand and talked as fast and joyously as I could. I told him about Sammy Jo starting pre-school and telling the teacher what the rules should be. I told him about all the flowers blooming in our new garden, the one he built for me in the spring, and how I had big bouquets of snapdragons and daisies in the kitchen window. I told him how big and round Sarah was, how humorously pregnant she was at eight-and-a-half months. How Morgan liked blowing bubbles, and how Alex had made an important play in the first basketball game of her senior year, and how Johnny loved seventh-grade football.

Tracy kept his eyes on me, smiling, and at every funny place the corners of his mouth turned up just a little more.

"I need to leave now. It's way past visiting hours. They let me stay longer because I got here late, but now I need to go. I'll be back in the morning." I hated to go.

"I'm going to kiss you goodbye now." I leaned over the bed railing and kissed him on his smiling lips. I kissed him four times. And each time, he kissed me back.

He could not speak or laugh or even move really, but he could kiss back. And he could smile. And he still knew what was funny.

That smile was good medicine. Perhaps not for him; he was by then beyond the reach of any cure, even the best. But it was the most excellent of treatments for my breaking heart.

That was the last time Tracy was awake in any meaningful way. After that, he opened his eyes for no more than ten or fifteen seconds at a time: one look, one partial smile, and he would sink back into sleep.

The day after my "conversation" with Tracy in MICU, the new doctor in charge sat down with me and Michelle in a small consultation room with no windows. She closed the door, and we sat on blue upholstered couches in soft lighting.

"The reality is that after seven weeks in the hospital, with all the best care and all the right antibiotics, Tracy is no better," she said, looking straight at me.

The room seemed to press in all around me. I put my hand on the couch to steady myself.

"The pneumonia has filled the right lung completely and is beginning to destroy the tissue," she continued. "The likelihood that the lung can recover is very slim."

"Can you live with just one lung?" I asked, still grasping for a shred of hope.

"Yes, some patients can live with one lung," she admitted in a calm and measured voice. "But there is pneumonia in the other lung, too. And Tracy's heart is so weak now that, even if everything else was stable and the left lung recovered completely, it is unlikely that he could ever manage the effort of breathing on his own with one lung."

The meaning of her words sank in slowly.

She went on: "We can go on treating him the way that we have been. That is the easiest course of action. It's what we are trained to do as doctors. And maybe, if we're lucky, in a month or two we might get the infection under control enough that he could go to a nursing home.

"But he is vulnerable to new infection at any time. That's been the pattern all summer. We get the infection partially controlled—then it recurs in a new round of infection."

The ups and downs of the summer flashed through my mind. Time and again, Tracy started to get better. "He is still critically ill," one of the doctors would report, "but he is inching in the right direction." They would begin the process of weaning him off the ventilator—and then there would be a new set-back.

I glanced at Michelle, then back at this new doctor.

"Will he ever come home?" I asked.

"No," she said, answering a litle too quickly I thought. But she was gentle. "I don't think he will ever be able to live at home." The doctor closed the fat medical notebook in her lap and folded her hands quietly on top of it.

"You need to decide what you want us to do," she said, "and what you think Tracy would want to do. Let me know what you decide." She shook hands with me and with Michelle. Then she left, closing the door behind her. Michelle and I stood in silence.

No breathing on his own. No talking. No coming home. No living free of machines.

No talking. No conversation. No coming home to our house, to me.

"So much to live for," he had said. It seemed a lifetime ago.

I would have called my other daughters and Tracy's brother and sister, but they were already on the way.

I don't recommend avoiding the subject of end-of-life questions; but I will always be glad we didn't get to the rest of those papers at the beginning of the summer. Even knowing the eventual outcome of Tracy's struggle against the pseudomonas bacteria, the enemy he was battling all along, I would not give up a single moment of that difficult summer.

Because I had an understanding employer and nine years' worth of accumulated sick leave, I was able to spend many days with him in Columbus. And because we had good health insurance, we had the "luxury" of fighting; the summer was not a financial catastrophe. Under other circumstances, everything might have been very different.

In any case, when the time came, it didn't matter whether or not we had the paperwork. I knew how Tracy would answer the hardest questions. I knew the things he could not live without. Chief among them was hope.

Do This in Remembrance of Me

After Tracy's death, I received a sympathy card from one of my Adrian Dominican friends with a quote on the front by Victor Hugo, the 19th century French novelist: "To love another is to touch the face of God."

In the Broadway musical "Les Miserables," based on Hugo's masterpiece of the same name, there is a similar line: "To love another person is to see the face of God." Tracy and I had seen the show together, and I always wondered if Hugo actually wrote something like that or if the line came strictly from the lyricist. Now I had my answer.

Over Tracy's last few years, that line had echoed in my mind. Through the challenging year after his pancreas transplant, through two-and-a-half years of dialysis as he hoped for a second kidney transplant, through heart problems and persistent nausea and the painful loss of fingers, I would think of those words, feel them, and hear them sung powerfully and passionately on an old tape of "Les Miz" that I kept in my car: *To love another person is to see the face of God.*

After Tracy's death, the words morphed in meaning as the song replayed itself, over and over, in my head: To love someone is to love God. God is in the love I still feel for Tracy. God is love. God is the person I loved and long for. Love is prayer. Even remembered love is prayer. I wasn't sure what I meant by any of it, or what it meant to me, but I was feeling all those things.

At home, the day before the funeral, I awoke from a dream in tears. I made my way to the family room where Mom and Dad, here from Maine to support me, were just waking up on the pull-out couch. I was 54 years old, but at that moment I was a little girl again, turning to my mother for comfort. I sat on the edge of the bed, weeping, and sobbed out the story of my dream.

"He was there! It was him, it was Tracy, in his ratty blue jeans and that old yellow polo shirt. He was leaning against something, a tree maybe, and he had his legs crossed the way he always did, and he had a hose or something in one hand. He was waving the hose very gently, sprinkling water on a baby boy—a toddler, or maybe an infant. The baby was inside a ball of light, all white and shining, and he was happy, playing and kind of rolling around in the light. And he did a kind of happy baby laugh each time Tracy sprinkled water on the ball of light.

"I came running up, on my way to somewhere, I don't know where, and I saw Tracy and I just stopped. He looked up and he smiled right at me. He didn't come toward me, and I didn't go toward him, but he smiled at me, and then he flipped the hose so a little of the water would fall on me. Like he was teasing me, or loving me, or something. And he was smiling.

"Then Sarah came running and went right past. She didn't see Tracy or the ball of light or anything. And then I said, 'I have to go. I have to buy a blue jacket for Sarah's baby when he comes.'

"Then I woke up. And he was gone.

"But he was there, in my dream. And he smiled at me."

Mom held me close as I rocked back and forth in grief, so happy to have "seen" him, so crushed to have had to wake up without him.

A few days later, I described the dream again, this time to Sister Jody, an Adrian Dominican colleague and friend. "You know what that means, don't you?" she said gently. "It means Tracy has already met Sarah's baby. He's watching over him until he's born."

No, I hadn't known that, and I wasn't sure I believed it, but I wrapped my arms gratefully around her interpretation.

The baby was born two-and-a-half weeks after Tracy's death. I did buy him a blue jacket, just as I'd promised in the dream. I knew he was to be named Ty, but Sarah and her husband surprised me with the announcement that their son would share his grandfather's middle name. Tracy's middle name. He would be Ty Regan.

Sometime after that, I joined a few friends for the Adrian Dominican Sisters' weekly Peace Prayer. I had not attended this service before, but I was seeking comfort anywhere I could find it, and this seemed like a good source. I couldn't sing; singing too quickly became weeping. And I found it hard to concentrate on the service. But the music and the stained glass windows above and around me were, indeed, therapeutic even as tears escaped from the corners of my eyes. Not being Catholic, I never knew when to sit or stand; I just did what everyone else did. After a while, we stood again in prayer. I was grateful to be able to close my eyes and bow my head. I hated drawing attention to myself by crying.

Suddenly, I felt water on my head and on my face; not tears but cool, gentle drops of water. I looked up to see Sister Jody sprinkling holy water on the congregants. *Holy water.*

I had felt that water before. I knew it without a doubt. I had felt it in my dream, when Tracy flicked the hose at me, sending water droplets through the air in mysteriously gentle arcs to fall on my face. Holy water in a holy dream.

The memory of my dream became even more precious.

For a while, when I prayed, I didn't know if I was talking to God or to Tracy or to both of them at the same time. When I closed my eyes, I felt—or imagined—Tracy being right there, with whatever or whoever God is, listening. Sometimes, in the middle of a prayer at church, with my head bowed, I could almost feel Tracy sitting next to me or standing behind me or even sometimes hovering above me. These visions, as I called them, always felt holy, even though I knew they weren't real, at least not in the physical sense.

I prayed for more dreams of Tracy (though they came very rarely) and for those Sunday morning visions; anything that made it seem like Tracy was near. I prayed for spiritual connection. Sitting down to dinner alone at my kitchen table, I often spoke aloud to God, fervently hoping there *was* a God, giving thanks for the meal, yes, but more often thanking Him for the gift of Tracy, the gift of having had him in my life, and pleading for another dream, another "visit."

For well over a year after Tracy's death, I could not sing in church. All the hymns made me cry now. Regardless of the church I was in or the hymn chosen, the words seemed written specifically about Tracy and me; and the music itself opened the floodgates of my emotions. I mouthed the words in silence, wiping my eyes, trying to be invisible. I never came to church without Kleenex. But I came, week after week, finding sanctuary in solitude as I sat in the sacred space, alone (I needed to be alone) but surrounded by fellowship.

Communion Sundays were the worst. And the best. When I heard the words, "This is my body, broken for you," I saw Tracy's body in my mind and could not stop the tears; and when we came forward to dip the bread into the wine, I could not speak, not even the simple response, "Amen." But I cherished communion for its words of ritual encouragement: "Do this in remembrance of me." And it was Tracy I remembered—kneeling at the communion rail with me, even when it was so difficult for him and they would gladly have served him standing; guiding me back to the pew with the light touch of his hand on my back; then sitting next to me, hands folded, remembering his mother, later his dad, perhaps confessing silently to selfishness, always giving thanks for the blessings in our life. That was the gift of remembrance communion gave me. I hoped it was not sacrilegious. It felt sacred. *To love another person is to see the face of God.*

I participated in a three-month grief group at Epworth and began to make a few new friends at the church. I participated in a follow-up spiritual discussion workshop and then helped lead a new grief group.

From others who had lost loved ones, I learned that many people find comfort in some special sign or unexpected circumstance that makes them feel their loved one is near. One couple, whose daughter died of cancer during her freshman year in college, felt a special connection to her any time they found a penny on the ground: pennies from heaven. With surprise, I realized I had a special token, too: the sun, on those occasions when it shone with white light. That quality of sunlight is fleeting and unpredictable; it never lasts long. But you can look directly at a white sun. For months, I had instinctively smiled whenever I saw that kind of sun; and often, especially if I were alone in my car or looking out a window at home, I would call to Tracy while gazing at the white sun: "Hi, honey."

It came to me then: the white sun was just like that shining ball of white light in my dream, when a baby boy chortled in pure delight and my husband smiled while flicking holy water on my face.

The white sun always takes me by surprise. And I still say hello to Tracy.

In my spare time, during the first year without Tracy, I made scrapbooks for my three daughters about their father and his family history. The project gave me a good reason to sort through the boxes I had only recently acquired following my father-in-law's death and the sale of the Church family farm.

Going through old photos, holding old newspaper clippings, reading Tracy's old high school essays, handling things that were part of his life long before I ever met him—all while trying to find just the right way to memorialize each daughter's unique relationship with her dad—was a prayerful reflection on his life and mine. I laughed and smiled and sometimes cried, cutting photos and paper and making beautiful pages. It felt holy and healing.

To love another person is to see the face of God.

Another sympathy card I received after Tracy's death came from a member of the Epworth congregation, a man Tracy had known through business long before we joined the church and whom we had greeted casually many times, before or after the Sunday service. This card came with a letter, in which this old business friend of Tracy's assured me that I would one day see Tracy again, just as this man would one day be reunited with a daughter who had died young. The letter was stunning in its caring and sensitivity, and in its certainty about the hereafter. It was a comforting message and it was unusual, because it offered such a straightforward and literal reference to the afterlife.

As time went by, I realized that hardly anyone talks about the afterlife. I guess it's not surprising: no one really knows what happens after death. Eternal life is a basic tenet of Christianity, but most people are not inclined to speculate aloud about what that really means. Even in the wonderful grief group I joined at the church, we never discussed what or where "life after death" might be; we focused on surviving in and making sense of this world. But I really felt Tracy's presence—or perhaps I just felt his absence—and I wanted to think more about death and life and the spirit and what might possibly come next.

I began reading anything I could find about death and love and faith. It was not research or study, and certainly not a disciplined theological search; it was just a serendipitous exploration, fueled by grief and longing, through whatever resources I stumbled upon and was drawn to.

I bought a book for fifty cents at the Siena Heights library book sale, about a Catholic woman's journey through the unexpected death of her new husband; I came to understand and appreciate the comfort she found in the rituals and rites of the Roman Catholic Church.

Another book, by a famous intellectual, chronicled the sudden death of the author's long-time husband and her efforts to make sense of that loss. I understood her need to evaluate and revisit, again and again, every moment of her husband's split-second end of life.

I read about another woman who responded to her husband's accidental death by becoming a Unitarian minister. I read a picture book about "cooking" your grief into a rich, savory, healing "soup" of memories. At the suggestion of my daughter, who was going through her own difficulties, I read a contemporary Christian novel about finding a new understanding of God through the tragic death of a child.

I read essays about angels and a delightful poem that announced, "everyone is right, as it turns out. You go to the place you always thought you would go." As we go through our daily lives, said Billy Collins in his poem titled "The Afterlife," "the dead of the day are...moving off in all imaginable directions, each according to his own private belief." I liked that.

I bought a book by Siena Heights professor Tad Dunne, who observed that "believers of all stripes bear the hope that whatever 'happened' to Jesus after his crucifixion might possibly happen to us, despite our radical and enduring ignorance of what that happening might be." I found comfort in this former priest's statement that "faith judges that nothing of value in our lives will be lost. Faith rests in the simple assurance that God loves each person now and will not let any person be utterly abolished." That made sense to me.

I read and thought and wrote, sometimes cried, and read some more. I got something from everything. Love and loss, grief and strength, memory and imagination: they all seemed tied together, somehow, in this journey of and through faith.

To love another person is to see the face of God.

For the last six months of his life, maybe even longer, Tracy wore a big black hard-plastic boot over his one remaining foot.

At night, his prosthetic leg, still wearing an athletic shoe, stood against the wall by our bed, right next to the knee-high black boot. Together, they suggested an eerie two-legged topless body that took grandchildren by surprise on weekend visits when they wandered in to find Grandma and Grampa in the morning.

The molded black boot had replaced the strap-on brace when another innocent blister, rubbed raw who knows how, appeared on Tracy's foot. The boot provided support for his ankle, heavy-duty protection for his foot, and space for the blister as it slowly, slowly, slowly tried to heal. As any diabetic patient should know, and as every long-term diabetic eventually learns, foot care is a critical part of maintaining good health; diabetics ignore it at their peril. Having lost one leg already, Tracy took the care of his remaining foot very seriously, even when it meant abruptly ending a long-planned bird hunting expedition, or a fishing trip, or even casual walks around the yard. The doctor didn't even need to say, "Stay off your foot for a couple of weeks." He knew.

We hadn't known at the beginning. The first time around, in the months leading up to our wedding, when the doctor said, "Try to stay off your foot," we thought he meant, "Don't run a marathon." Well, that advice was easy enough to follow: Tracy just did small errands, small projects around the house, no hiking. But in fact, what the doctor meant by "Try to stay off your foot" was: "Do not use that foot *at all.* Use crutches. Balance on your other leg." By now, we knew what happened when you didn't take the doctor's advice seriously.

So when a small raw spot appeared on his foot, some time that last year, Tracy went immediately to the foot doctor and ended up with this storm-trooper-type boot. This was a big improvement over crutches. Since the raw spot was on the side of his foot, not the bottom, he was free to walk; the boot's big molded foot box with its carefully sculpted and padded interior would protect the foot and the wound for the months-long healing process.

That was just one part of the treatment, however. In addition, he was to soak the foot morning and evening, dry it carefully, use moisturizing cream to keep the skin supple, then carefully roll a clean sock over the foot and up to the knee. None of this was new; he'd been there, done that, plenty of times in the past. But this time was different. By now Tracy's hands were in bad shape. He already had lost several fingers and he felt excruciating pain in the blackening tips of several other fingers any time they bumped a counter or a doorknob. Holding a pen to record his daily meds was difficult enough. He simply could not massage lotion into his calf or manipulate a tall sock onto his foot, over his heel and up to his knee.

This time, foot care would be a two-person job.

At first, we both railed against the demands of this regimen. Tracy had always been proud and independent, and it was hard for him to accept yet one more example of helpless dependence on others, even if the "other" was me; it made him irritable and short sometimes. For me, it was hard to fit this fifteen- or twenty-minute process into an early morning schedule that already began at 5:00 a.m. in order to get Tracy to dialysis in Toledo by 6:45, and me to work at Siena Heights by 8:00. And at night, I would be dead on my feet, or half asleep in a chair, when we suddenly remembered: time for Tracy to soak his foot.

Why? I would sigh to myself. Why do we have to do this? I knew the answer, of course. We both did. And so we did it.

But over time, over those last months, something changed. Perhaps we got the routine down better. Perhaps we both let go of our frustrations with this necessary interruption in our mornings and evenings. Perhaps we both sensed that our time together might be limited. But neither of us could have admitted that.

However it happened, the annoyance disappeared on both sides. Those morning and evening rituals became not an intrusion or a burden but a gift—something tender and overwhelmingly intimate; something almost holy.

One early morning, kneeling in the circle of light from the lamp behind the easy chair where Tracy sat, I pushed the basin of water away and gently toweled Tracy's foot. When it was dry, I reached into the jumbo jar of moisturizer for a scoop of skin cream and began massaging his foot, his ankle, his calf. I worked slowly and gently, caressing his skin and looking up at his face now and then as we talked quietly. It came to me then that this, indeed, was learning and growing, loving and respecting, helping and asking for help, just as we had promised on our wedding day. Maybe we talked about Tracy's dialysis friends, whose big hearts and big challenges always made him humble and grateful. Maybe we talked about what I would do at work, or what might taste good for dinner that night. I don't really remember what we discussed. But I do remember realizing that this touching, this sharing, was as sensual, as powerful and as fulfilling as any physical connection had ever been.

And I felt, like never before, the impact and meaning of some of the New Testament stories. Martha, busy with cooking and in need of help, is annoyed when Mary just sits at Jesus' feet and listens. The meal can wait, Jesus suggests; sometimes it is more important to set aside the demands of daily life and just listen, calm your spirit, open your soul. In another story, another Mary anoints Jesus' feet with expensive oil; one of the apostles complains that the oil could have been sold to help the needy. Relax, Jesus seems to say: You will have more time to help the poor, but you will not always have me.

Fingers and palms slippery with skin cream, I massaged Tracy's foot and leg and reflected. There would be more time for the other duties of life; but these moments were precious and fleeting. The one who washes another's feet kneels in service, becoming a servant to the other. And yet, there is vulnerability for one who puts his or her body—even just a foot—in the hands of another. The two must trust each other. We trusted each other, and opened ourselves to something more.

Later, I thought about how that twice-daily ritual enriched our last months together at home, and how much intimacy it brought into that fragile time.

This is my body broken for you.
Do this in remembrance of me.
To love another person is to see the face of God.

It's not deep theology. But for me, it was comfort and healing. For me, it was faith.

Letters From the Lonesome Valley

> This is my Father's world, and to my listening ears
> All nature sings and round me rings
>   The music of the spheres.
> This is my Father's world: I rest me in the thought
> Of rocks and trees, of skies and seas;
>   His hand the wonders wrought.

This is My Father's World" was one of Tracy's and my favorite hymns. A shared love of the outdoors was one of the things that first brought us together and the images in that hymn spoke directly to our sense of the presence of God in the natural world. So it was one of the hymns I chose for Tracy's funeral, although on that day it spoke to me not about God's world, but about my world and my husband's world, the world we had hiked in, hunted in, kissed in. I had always found the images so beautiful, but that day, at the funeral, I struggled to choke out the words; and when we reached the next verse, I gave up. I mouthed the words silently, in tears: "In the waving grass, I hear him pass. He is with me everywhere."

I certainly felt he was with me everywhere. Tracy. With me and not with me. Everywhere and nowhere. His absence was ever-present.

Losing Tracy was the hardest thing I had ever faced, harder than any of his amputations or surgeries, harder than my own breast cancer, harder (for me) than any of our daughters' life difficulties. Tracy's death on August 30, 2004, shook me to the core and left me walking in the "lonesome valley."

I don't know what I thought that beautiful gospel song meant when I sang the words at summer camp in the 1960s: "You must walk this lonesome valley. You have to walk it by yourself. Oh, nobody else can walk it for you. You have to walk it by yourself."

But I knew when I found myself there: walking through my house wailing, walking through my days overwhelmed by sadness, walking through my memories alone, bereft. Walking by myself.

I was in the lonesome valley.

I wondered how, or if, I would ever leave that sad place. And what would it mean if I did? If I became less sad, would it mean I loved my husband less? Would it mean I had forgotten him? Betrayed him? As had happened so often in Tracy's last weeks and months, I found, when he was gone, that I did not know what to pray for, could not think what to hope.

His death was not a surprise to most people. A well-meaning colleague even said to me at the funeral home, "I suppose at some level it must be a relief." The comment took my breath away. Others may have expected his death, but I had expected him to live, to make it, to beat this thing. I did not expect him to die; not until the last day, when I had to make the decision to help him along. I was glad, then, that he died so quickly, within minutes after we stopped the oxygen. Then I knew his care truly had become life support. His body could not live any longer.

It had been a long hard summer of driving back and forth, talking and reading aloud to him, encouraging and cheerleading, hoping and praying; moments of encouragement, days of despair. But through it all, I always had Tracy: to visit, to care about, to love. I had the hope of his smile, his wink, his kissing me back. And then...I had none of that.

So, no, it was not a relief, not on any level. It was terrible.

And so began my walk in the lonesome valley.

I had never discussed with Tracy the bargain I proposed to God before our marriage, more of a plea than a pre-nup: *Just give us five good years and I will be satisfied.* But I suspect he had his own agreement with the Almighty.

He knew, long before I met him, that there was no certainty about the future. After decades of diabetes, he was well aware of the possibilities for medical mayhem. Dialysis and the kidney transplant before we were married, and the amputation soon after the wedding, were unavoidable reminders of that deadly potential. And over the fourteen years of our marriage, he confronted an amazing array of problems and complications, all related in some way to diabetes.

But despite all that, Tracy was not a sickly person. That was *his* bargain with God: "Throw at me what you must; I'll endure it. Just let me live an active life."

And he did.

He ran a business, designing and building complex hydraulic machines for clients that ranged from the U.S. Army to major automakers to an independent environmental design firm. He worked on his skeet shooting average with a passion, fished every summer, bird hunted every fall, and experimented with gourmet cooking whenever he brought home wild game. He read books, wrote short stories, and cheered the Tigers, Pistons and Red Wings. He was a regular at our daughters' volleyball and basketball games. He kept an eye on the house and the yard, argued politics, and made me laugh every day.

When declining health and the demands of his second stint on dialysis meant he could no longer keep reliable business hours, he accepted that difficult defeat with dignity; he closed his company of six years—and began building a remote-control airplane in our spare bedroom and a pair of Adirondack chairs in the back garage. And, still, he put on a sport coat for every doctor visit; he never wanted to look sick.

When medical appointments began to feel like the only thing on his schedule, he became the biggest fan of our grandchildren's athletic efforts, driving to the "away" basketball and football contests as well as the home games. When problems with his remaining foot, and his fingers, finally ended his ability to hunt and fish, he began reading philosophy and contemplated law school.

He simply refused to let illness define him.

He took his pills religiously, morning and evening, but his life— our life—was not about sickness. It was about enjoying every day, learning and growing as we had done from the start.

In July of 2003, a year before Tracy died, I wrote a letter to my parents, reporting on our annual week in northern Michigan with the girls and their families. It was our ninth summer at Chimney Corners, where everyone swam, the grandchildren flocked to the frog pond, and we all reconnected. But this year's vacation also included "vacation dialysis," so Tracy and I had traveled back and forth three times to a clinic sixty miles away. We did our best to turn those drives into tender together-time, although by then we never traveled without a plastic dishpan to deal with sudden and unexpected nausea. Even so, "it was a good week for us," I wrote to Mom and Dad:

> ...and good for our family, though not without its challenges
> as you know. Certainly, it was different this year for me and
> Tracy, but we're so glad we were able to go that any problems
> were worth it.

Tracy is lucky to get one good day out of every two, and a couple of his dialysis days up north were pretty trying ('dispiriting' might be a more accurate description of the effect on Tracy), but he is one tough character. Given even half an afternoon to focus on the 'good stuff,' he's got the will and fiber to withstand three or four more days of being battered by circumstance. I probably sound melodramatic, but it's tough stuff. A weaker person than Tracy would have succumbed by now—to deep depression if not far worse.

Through it all, he's still the light of my life: he makes me laugh at the most unexpected moments, he's my biggest fan (though you are contenders), and he's surely the great love that was written in the stars for me.

At some point, Tracy and I stumbled onto the gospel passage that became our *modus operandi*, Matthew 6:34: "Do not be anxious about tomorrow, for tomorrow will be anxious for itself. Let the day's own trouble be sufficient for the day."

Let the day's own trouble be sufficient for the day.

It was a good guide to getting by. Don't stress about tomorrow. Focus on today—its joys as well as its problems. And have a little faith. Most of the time, we managed: accepting the present, dealing with challenges one day at a time. We made a conscious effort to be grateful for each new morning—and for each other. We did it together.

But after Tracy's death, we weren't doing it together. Now it was just me, walking in the lonesome valley. And each "day's own trouble" was excruciating. I had no idea how to let it be "sufficient.".

During Tracy's long summer at OSU, I had started a journal to keep track of what was happening and monitor the ups and downs of each day. When he was gone, I kept writing. The writing became my lifeline. Writing about my anguish—putting it into words on paper—did not lessen the pain, but it did help me endure it. For a while I wrote every day, often three and four times a day.

Aug. 31—3:45 a.m.: I can't sleep. I am full of tears...

Sept. 4—6:30 a.m.: I just feel empty...

Sept. 6—6:45 a.m.: I am so glad Mother and Dad are staying on a few days. Being home alone will be so hard. I am a little afraid. This was never "my" house—it was always "ours"—and it is so full of Tracy, in every room, every corner, every cupboard, closet and bookshelf...

Sept. 7—10:30 p.m.: Back to work; a half day. It was okay, but all through the day the sadness built up until my cup runneth over with tears and grief. Dad just came in to give me a hug. I can't remember when I needed Mom and Dad so much...

Sept. 10: Home alone now. Everything seems to make me cry. I walk through the house, sobbing, calling out, "Honey! Honey!" I look everywhere for signs of Tracy's spirit... I never knew how deeply and consumingly I would miss him, and how painful would be the loss. This is so hard, so very hard...

Sept. 12: A hard day. A beautiful day. Tears and heartache that start in the gut, hot and burning. Honey, I miss you so.

Sept. 17: Some days aren't too bad; some are terrible from the moment I get up. Driving alone in the car is my saddest time. Sunsets, hawks, squirrels—they all remind me of Tracy. I call out for him so often in tears...

Sept. 24: What is heaven, really? What is the afterlife likely to be? How tangible is the spirit after death? Is the spirit everywhere, the way we think of God? I feel I have you with me all the time, Tracy—and not with me at all. Please—be real, be with me, love me...

Sept. 27: Four weeks since you died. I so want to know you are still with me in spirit, loving me, caring about me, ready to make me laugh if only I could hear you. I've lost all sense of time. It seems an eternity, and yet only a moment, since you gave me that big smile and kissed me goodnight at the hospital. Did you know it was goodbye? The past twenty years seem to telescope into a few fleeting moments, while the future looms like a great slow weight. Oh Tracy, I love you so much.

All that—and much, much more—was in the first four weeks.

Grief overwhelmed me with no warning, at unexpected times and in unexpected places.

When Tracy was alive, I used to zoom through the grocery store, collecting food and prescriptions with high-speed efficiency so I could get back home to enjoy the limited time we had together between my job and his appointments. After his death, grocery shopping became a much different undertaking: I took my time wandering the aisles, looking at new products, gazing at cuts of meat. There was no rush to get home to my empty house; and at least in my Foodtown, there were familiar faces. The check-out clerks smiled, recognizing a steady customer. The store pharmacists called me by name. "Hello, Mrs. Church. I'm so sorry about your husband." I had been one of their best customers for years, picking up Tracy's many monthly prescriptions. They were like family in a weird way. I made a point of watching for them and waving, even though I had no reason, now, to stop at the pharmacy counter.

One day, navigating my grocery cart past the baking supplies, turning into a new aisle, I found myself staring at the neatly packed shelves of canned corn and green beans and tomatoes. Suddenly, I was weeping uncontrollably, because...because...because I no longer needed to stock up on canned vegetables (better for Tracy because they delivered less potassium than fresh produce) or stuffed olives (way too salty, but always his favorite guilty pleasure). The tears came in a rush. I tried to hide my face. How could I explain crying over canned peas?

A few aisles later, I was wiping my eyes again, wishing I still needed those high-priced cans of "Boost"—vanilla only, thank you—the nutritional supplement that had kept Tracy going even when he could not eat.

Ambushed by grief.

It happened at work, too. In my job, I talk to many people every day. I'm on the phone a lot. One day, with my desk in its typical state of disarray, the phone rang. I reached over a pile of papers toward the receiver—then froze, my hand in mid-air as the phone rang and rang. And suddenly, I was weeping, knowing it didn't matter who was calling. All that mattered was...it wasn't Tracy. And it would never be Tracy calling, never again. Never would my workday be brightened by the sound of his voice on the other end of the line. "Hi." That quick and unexpected hello that had always worked a golden magic on any day that he called.

No, it was not Tracy. I covered my face with both hands as the call went into voice mail. Ambushed by grief.

It happened often in the car: Looking up on a bright clear day to see a small plane overhead and hearing Tracy's voice speculate on whether it was a "homebuilt." Driving down a country road and realizing I couldn't remember the stories he had told me about roaming these particular fields as a boy. Hearing a new country song that hit an emotional nerve...

The first time Keith Urban's "Making Memories of Us" came on my car radio, I had to swerve to the side of the road. Half-way home from the grocery store on a sunny Saturday, I put the car in park and wept while I listened. I had no idea who was singing, but whoever it was, he was channeling Tracy Church directly to me:

> I'm gonna be here for you, baby.
> I'll be a man of my word.
> Speak the language in a voice
> that you have never heard...

That seemed to be just what Tracy was doing. Speaking to me in some secret silent voice, still keeping his promises, keeping our vows.

...there'll be a new day
coming your way.

I'm gonna be here for you from now on;
this you know somehow.
You've been stretched to the limit
but it's alright now.

"Stretched to the limit..." That was how it felt. Tracy would know that, and would be so sorry to know that he was the cause. Then came the kicker:

...If there's life after this,
I'm gonna be there to meet you
with a warm wet kiss.

Everything about that song seemed to speak specifically to me, and about Tracy and me. I went out and bought the CD immediately. I played it often, even though it made me cry.

From day to day, there was no predicting when grief would abruptly suck the breath from my chest, leaving my heart and lungs heaving in ragged despair. I wondered how it was possible to make so many tears.

The first holidays and anniversaries came and went. For several months, every Monday around three o'clock in the afternoon I marked another week without him here on earth. On the opening day of pheasant season, all day I wanted to be outdoors, sure I would feel his presence.

Hosting my first Thanksgiving without him, surrounded by my girls and grandchildren and in-laws, I said grace aloud, giving thanks for all the gifts we shared, especially Tracy, without whom I would not have had any of that family around me. I made it through the grace, barely, then looked down to find my hands shaking uncontrollably.

Eventually, I began writing letters to Tracy. Yes, letters.

We had written many letters to each other through the years, through the painful early times of distance and separation and struggle, and then again while I worked in Ohio after we were married. Even when we were not apart, we often gave each other cards and little notes. Now my journal became a letter-book, a one-sided correspondence.

"Now that we are again apart," I wrote in the first letter, "I think it would help me to write to you, to ask your help in figuring out my anguish and learning how to be, how to feel, how to cry (I don't need much help there), how to go on without you."

Just after New Year's, four months into that first year alone, everything caught up with me. I wrote to Tracy about it:

> I woke up at 5:00 this morning and began thinking about our last times curled together in our bed, before the transplant and then during that brief time at home before the pneumonia took you back to the hospital. And I began weeping uncontrollably. I wept and wept, and got more Kleenex, and finally got up at 7:00 and wept while washing my face and while brushing my teeth. Now I sit at the kitchen table, with coffee in my Santa mug, from the set you gave me. I'm not crying anymore, but I have the chair pulled out for you to join me...

I could almost see him in that chair, in jeans and his black down vest: long legs crossed in his usual way, one arm on the table, a quirky wry smile on his face.

As time went by, I "managed" my days and weeks in a way that made people say I was "doing well" but grief was my constant companion: the empty outline of the real companion I missed so much. Tears were never far below the surface. And even though I never felt closer to my absent husband than when I cried, the weeping began to worry me.

In March, I wrote to Tracy: "Six months you have been gone.

Fully one half a year. I can't grasp it. I can't stand it. These last few days have been as hard as any since you died. It just does not get easier. I do fine for a while and then—boom. An explosion of missing you burns in my insides, in my gut, in my jaw. And recently my grief has frightened me. It has felt like I was on the edge of some kind of madness."

Going to work Monday through Friday, forcing myself to interact with the living world, helped keep the madness at bay. On weekends, going to church became both an opportunity to let grief out, often weeping silently by myself in the pew, and a chance to let people in. Exchanging even a few words with friends and acquaintances, or just greeting the pastor at the end of the service, provided vital reassurance that I was, in fact, keeping it together.

Grandchildren helped, too.

"Sammy Jo is coming in an hour to spend the night, and I am grateful," I wrote one Saturday morning early in that first spring. "This would be a bad day to be by myself." At the end of that day, I reported our grandmother-granddaughter adventures to Tracy:

> Sammy is singing and playing in the bathtub. It is good she is here. She's keeping me sane today. We went to the newly renovated Bedford Library to pick out a book. The library is beautiful now; you would like it. But I almost cried, even with Samantha, when I saw a man who looked so much like you, sitting in the library and reading. I started to go closer, approaching him, before stopping myself. What did I think? That he could become you?
>
> When we came home, Sammy rode the tricycle in the driveway. And then, at her suggestion, we got out the coaster and she went sliding on the north side of the house where the snow hasn't quite melted. Imagine—bicycling and snow sliding on the same day! You would have enjoyed it so much...
>
> I could cry a lot. Thank heaven for Sammy.

Having the "grands" with me for a night or a weekend always reminded me of Tracy's lasting imprint on my life; and they filled my days with laughter and focus, as toddlers and pre-schoolers naturally do. They were curious, too, and asked me often about Grampa Tracy and Doggie Jess, both of whom had left my life, and their lives, at about the same time. Where were they now, the kids wanted to know. Why had they gone away? I tried to be honest about death in a non-scary way, while sharing my own faith that, somehow, in some way, some part of them lived on. A book from the library about the mythical death of a mythical pet dinosaur helped us talk about sadness and about missing the people or dogs (or dinosaurs) who were no longer with us. I read the book aloud several times, for myself as much as for the little ones.

I told them my own stories, too, to help them remember their grandfather. "Grampa always made the pancakes before," I said to DJ and Morgan one Saturday morning, tying on an apron and summoning as much sparkle as I could. "I guess I better learn how now!" My efforts, producing Mickey Mouse pancakes with two round ears on a round head, were well-received and happily consumed.

That same night, I called DJ and Morgan to the window to hear the eerie, unmistakeable hoot of an owl in the dark woods behind our house. "Grampa Tracy probably could have told you what kind of owl that is," I said, wishing he were there, secretly wondering if he was. "Tomorrow we'll see if we can find a book about owls." And we did.

Those weekends with grandchildren were more than just fun. They were therapeutic—emotionally, psychologically, even physically. In the nicest way, the little ones reminded me to cook and eat meals, clean the house, do the laundry, laugh, take care of others.

Even on weekends without the grandchildren, I found myself reviewing the details of those sometimes long and lonely days in my journal. Writing became a coping mechanism, another way to reassure myself of my sanity. I'm okay, I seemed to be telling myself (and Tracy) in the journal entries: Just look at what I did today.

What I did was sometimes as simple as learning to put staples in Tracy's antique stapler, sorting through medical bills, finding my way for the first time alone to the recycling center, or talking with my daughters. But in "telling Tracy" about these simple things, I came to understand my own feelings.

"This afternoon I visited the stable for the first time in a long while," I wrote one Saturday evening. (I had stopped my after-work riding lessons sometime after Tracy went back on dialysis, when health problems began keeping him home alone all day). "There was lots of activitiy at the barn on this gorgeous day," I told him:

> Everyone was preparing for tomorrow's jumping derby. I talked for a while with my old instructor, Meg—told her about everything that has happened. Told her about my fear, now, of riding, because there would be no one at home to call if I fell off and got hurt.
>
> Isn't that strange? I have fallen so many times and we never called you; I just got back on and kept riding. But now it feels scary. What if something happened? I would be alone. Whenever I decide to go back to riding, I'll start slow. Until I feel strong.

The habit of recounting my steps, listing my activities as a way to find the meaning in my days, had begun when Tracy first went back to the hospital and was unable to talk with me. After the first week, one of the doctors had taken me aside and offered a few words of advice: "Be sure you go out during the day—shop, talk to friends. And make sure you leave at night and get some rest." His message was gentle but firm: It would not help Tracy, or me, if I became a nervous wreck.

I took the doctor's suggestion; and a few evenings later I reviewed my day, writing in the present tense—which even now brings back the feeling I had then of living inside a bubble:

I park further away from the hospital to get more exercise. I stop for breakfast and linger, enjoying my coffee. I feel guilty.

I find Tracy in a sedated slumber. Does he dream? The doctors want him to sleep, the nurse says. Then she draws blood for more cultures. Always more cultures.

I talk to Tracy, remind him I'm there, tell him to keep sleeping and just breathe. I make a new sign for the end of his bed, with the date, my love and a big smiling sun—in case he opens his eyes and can focus.

I read in silence. And then, suddenly, a strangled gurgling cry comes from his throat. Silence. Then another horrible gurgle. The nurse assures me all is well—the explanation has to do with the air balloon around the breathing tube. No alarms go off. But he continues to make these awful sounds. I tell the nurse I'll wait outside for a while—the sounds are too scary. And why haven't I heard them before? The nurse says they will re-adjust and re-tape the breathing tube.

I meet with the doctors and fall apart. The reality is Tracy hasn't made much progress. He had progressed, and then he went backwards a little last night, hence all the adjustments with the respirator. The doctors are nice, really, and they know what they are doing. I just wish I didn't dissolve each time I talked with them.

I leave for a while and shop: a doctor's kit for Sammy Jo's fourth birthday. How appropriate.

I go back to the hospital and read my book: *West With the Night* by Beryl Markham. Beautifully written and full of words no one uses anymore: 'vaingloriously' and others I can't recall.

I do the crossword puzzle, talking to Tracy all the while, hoping he hears me. I end up with most of the puzzle done but six random squares empty. How can that be?

I talk with the nurse. Today's is Allison, who comes from Minnesota and misses the 'land of 10,000 lakes.'

I come home—to the motel—and drink a beer while watching a TV special about the changing role and opportunities for women in sports. I cry.

Somehow, just recording those mundane activities confirmed to me that, yes, I was alive and living that day, even if I felt like an empty shell going through the motions.

The same was true on those lonely weekends, months later, as I struggled to find my footing in a world without Tracy by writing letters to him in a journal he would never see.

It would be nice to say that faith comforted me every step of the way on that lonesome journey, but that was not the case. At the beginning, and for quite some time, faith was no help.

I never lost faith. From the moment Tracy died, arms uplifted, silently calling "Mom, Mom," I was sure his spirit lived on, somehow, somewhere. But that was not much comfort, or even any comfort at all. Believing that his spirit was *somewhere* simply did not help in understanding that he, himself, was *nowhere*. And I could not grasp that reality—that he was nowhere on the earth, that he would never come back to share another sunny day, or hopeful sunrise, or funny story, or any moment at all. I knew it in my brain, of course, but my heart and my senses kept forgetting. And each time I encountered that vacuum pressing in on me, it took my breath away, literally. Again and again.

"I want to believe you are 'alive' in some eternal life," I wrote to him. "I want to know you are with me all the time, the way the Sisters say. I want that faith. But I can't feel it. Someday, maybe it will comfort me to know you are 'in a better place,' but for now, all I can see and feel is that my place—my world, our world, our home—is a much sadder place and so very empty."

A year after the New Year's day meltdown when I cried for so long, as I started a second new year, I went on a date. By then, Tracy had been gone for sixteen months. It seemed like I should try. So when the invitation came, I said yes.

"It was okay," I wrote the next day, "and fun, sort of. But I felt... nothing. Nothing at all, except that by the end of the evening I knew he had to leave fast so I could cry. I came in, locked the door, collapsed against it and began to wail. And now, all day today, I have cried on and off, missing you so much.

"What would you want me to do, Tracy? I am certain, actually, that you would want me to be happy. But how? In what way? As a grandmother? As a mother? As an alumni director? As a widow? As a woman?"

In my Christmas message to family and friends a few weeks earlier, I had written, "All is well. 'The light shines in the darkness and the darkness has not overcome it.' (John 1:5)"

"But I do not feel as self-assured as that sounds," I admitted after the Saturday night date, in one of my journal-letters to Tracy. "All is not easy, or clear or simple or serene. Sometimes all is a mess. But whatever all is, you are a precious part of it."

I was not ready for dating. Not yet. I wondered if I would ever be ready. Or if I would ever want to be ready.

A few months later, I stopped writing letters. There was no moment of decision, no conscious turning point. I just stopped writing to Tracy. My journal became, instead, what perhaps it had always been: a conversation with myself, where I questioned, debated and explored ideas and emotions. Inspiration came from many sources: Sunday sermons, my kids, dreams, the radio, even junk mail ("Tracy, we want you back" said a sale announcement from the local Jeep dealer). I still wrestled with memories, and reeled from lightning bolts of sadness and longing, but the world around me gradually became more interesting and inviting.

Driving to church one Sunday, I heard a comment on public radio that resonated so deeply with me that I had to write about it, because I knew I wanted to remember:

> The man being interviewed, referring to problems in Eastern Europe and the historical ethnic divisions there, commented that "isolation nurtures an obsession with the past." Wow. Isolation nurtures an obsession with the past. That is exactly why I must balance my desire for solitude with social interaction. Too much alone-time leads me into the misty past. I still believe it's important to go there sometimes—to treasure my memories, to make sense of them, to mine them for meaning and guidance. But I can't live there. I can't live in the past.

Isolation nurtures an obsession with the past.

I began reaching out more, making deliberate plans to be with people for some part of every weekend, and to get together with others after work once or twice a week. I began horseback riding again. Welcomed grandchildren for more weekend visits. Contacted old friends and tried to be open to meeting new ones.

"I have had an epiphany," I wrote, two years into life on my own:

> Driving to work, these thoughts crossed my mind: I could run for office. I could audition for a play. I could put an addition on my house. I could visit Great Smoky Mountain National Park—or the great migration in East Africa. And then it came to me: The first two years after Tracy's death were simply about survival. Now, at last, life is becoming about possibilities.

Grief had not gone away. It does not go away. But it no longer owned me.

Months later, I attended our daughter Cindy's baptism and confirmation into the Catholic Church. In her forties, she had found faith and a measure of peace. Moved by the power of that Easter Vigil service, I wrote in my journal, reflecting on my own spiritual journey:

> More and more, I think my experience years ago helping to rewrite the Epworth mission statement was pivotal for me. I think we produced what will always be my personal mission statement: *Give life meaning: Find a need and fill it. Find a hurt and heal it. Find your faith and share it.* The church has since rewritten their mission, adopting a more traditional charge to make disciples. But in my own life, I rely on that earlier version.

More months passed. I wrote less frequently. Soon the holidays were coming around once more. Just before Thanksgiving, another postcard arrived for Tracy from the Jeep dealer. Not so long ago, I would have cried to see this personalized junk mail, but this time I smiled: "Tracy!" the text called out. "Come home for the holidays! We miss you!"

"Not as much as I do, I'm pretty sure," I replied aloud in a cheery sing-song. I put the postcard—with its picture of a bright red Jeep, just like Tracy's except newer—up on the refrigerator with a Christmas magnet. "Yessirree, honey, you come home for the holidays. We do miss you," I said with a smile.

Sometime after that, there was more mail for Tracy, this time from the Secretary of State: "Renewal information enclosed. Open immediately." Oh, I thought: Tracy's driver's license. Adult licenses are good for ten years in Michigan; his was up for renewal. In bold red type, the letter inside shouted: "Avoid late fees! Check the expiration date!" This time I laughed out loud. "I believe I know the expiration date, Madame Secretary of State. But apparently you don't!" I chuckled all the way from the mailbox to my front door and into the kitchen, knowing how much Tracy would have enjoyed the humor. Laughter was still good medicine.

On May 31, 2009, as I approached the five-year anniversaries of everything related to Tracy's last summer and his losing battle with the pseudomonas bacteria, I went to church.

By now, Sunday mornings followed a familiar pattern: sleep a little later than usual, linger over morning coffee with a book or the Sunday paper, check the time, then frantically jump into my clothes and drive like a crazy person to get to church before the end of the opening hymn. Afterwards, I would catch up with a few friends over coffee in the church lobby, or breakfast at a local eatery, then drive home at a sensible speed, stopping for a few groceries and for a fill-up at the discount gas station. The Sunday morning routine provided comprehensive "refueling" for me and my Malibu, fortifying us both for the week ahead.

On this warm and sunny day, I came home with a full tank and settled onto the back porch to write in my journal:

> 'Come, Holy Spirit. Come.' That was the theme of today's sermon, Pentecost Sunday, all about the God of wind and fire. God came in the wind, in tongues of fire—not when anyone was expecting him/her, but when it was time. Wind like breath: 'Breathe on me, breath of God. Fill me with life anew.' We sang that hymn.

I thought about how that same hymn had come into my mind in the dawning hours of the day Tracy died: "Breathe on me, breath of God. Fill me with life anew." Then, on that sunny afternoon on my porch, I set the pen down. Closed the book. Took a deep breath, inhaling the sweet spring air.

I didn't realize it at the time, but that brief entry at the end of May, almost five years after Tracy's death, turned out to be the last time I wrote in the journal. The change came...not when anyone was expecting it, but when it was time. I had filled two complete books.

I kept writing, of course, but now I wrote poems, and sometimes essays. I wrote letters again—to living recipients who wrote (or more often called) back. I was out of the lonesome valley.

I had emerged from the really sad place several years before then, but the end of the journal made it official. I had walked the lonesome valley by myself. And survived.

Cindy gave me the journal at the beginning of Tracy's long stay at the Ohio State Medical Center. She bought it in the hospital gift store, and handed it to me, saying, "You need to write."

How did she know that?

I'll never know, just like I will never know what brought her to Ohio, to the hospital, that first morning in Columbus. She appeared unexpectedly like an angel, and sat down with me as I waited anxiously, wondering why the nurses would not let me in to see Tracy. Eventually, she and I went in together—and found Tracy with a breathing tube down his throat, recovering fearfully from cardiac arrest. Code Blue. The journal became my lifeline.

The journal came with a title, "Beacon of Light," and a picture of a lighthouse on the cover. Every few pages, there was a quotation at the top of the page. One of the first was this:

> I have often thought that the people who built lighthouses, and those who kept them, were optimists. A lighthouse is a beacon to all on the sea—a sure sign that land is near and that someone aloft is keeping a steadfast eye for their safe passage.
>
> (Fletcher Cairns)

When I first read those words, it was Tracy I thought about, wondering what to pray for, what even to hope for. Not knowing what lay ahead for him or for us, I wrote on that page:

> Safe passage. That's what I'll ask for: safe passage for Tracy to wherever he is going. I hope it's home, our home, and life as we love to share it, with books and flowers, ideas and humor and so much love.
>
> But if it's a new life he's headed toward, that life that is beyond and outside this world, I hope God grants him safe passage there, too, and a journey without too much pain. And I hope the afterlife is what we all dream about—bright and shining, a house of many mansions where a place is waiting for us, and where all the great loves of this life will surround and comfort him.

I will never know how painful that passage was for Tracy. The morning I wrote that entry, when I woke up early in a Columbus motel room, Tracy still had seven weeks to go in his journey. But I know how painful it was for me to go on without him. The journal was my beacon of light, and writing in it for almost five years helped with my safe passage—into, through and beyond the lonesome valley.

Life was still in transition. Maybe it always is. But I was back in a life of light and laughter.

Holding On and Letting Go

After all this time, Tracy's green bathrobe was still hanging on a hook at one end of our closet. The robe had been a Christmas gift back in 1994, replacing a red one I had inadvertently bleached in the wash. This "new" green one was overdue for replacement well before Tracy went into the hospital in 2004, but I made no move to retire it, even when Tracy did not come home. The heavy old terrycloth still pushed its way into the bedroom now and then, stopping the sliding closet door with a muffled thump; dressing for work in a hurry, I would stuff the fabric back into the closet, quickly pushing the door over to contain it.

There was a handkerchief folded in the bathrobe pocket. In the months following Tracy's death, every so often I reached into the pocket, pulled out the hanky and held it over my nose, inhaling the scent. Tracy's scent. The thin cotton, off-white from too many washings, held onto that familiar essence for a long time. I would breathe it in slowly, standing immobile, summoning the sense of him for a few moments, then return the hanky to its hiding place.

Some widows and widowers get rid of a spouse's clothing quickly, even immediately, after the loved one's death. Sometimes circumstances require it. And sometimes family members encourage that rapid purging, looking for a way, right now, to help the bereaved mother or father or sibling begin to recover. Some grievers appreciate that help.

But as in so many other experiences of grief, there is no one "right time" to move on in this particular way.

A friend of mine was grateful that her visiting daughters removed her husband's clothing the weekend of the funeral. Another friend quickly tackled the job herself, when it was too painful to encounter her husband's many shirts, pressed and lined up neatly, each time she entered the walk-in closet they had shared.

My mother, on the other hand, kept my father's trousers—the ones he wore to his volunteer job the day before he collapsed—folded over the upstairs banister for a year. She often fingered the material with love, grateful to remember that he had lived an active life until the end.

As for me, I did nothing with our closet for quite a while.

Seven months after Tracy's death, my school-teacher brother and his teenage daughter had come to visit during their spring break. We had a wonderful time together, tackling all kinds of undone handyman chores around the house: taking down a dead tree, clearing my front ditch, purchasing a small TV to bring voices into the bedroom, rerouting the cable to accommodate the bedroom TV. And then Sam had asked, "Shall we go through Tracy's clothes?"

Suddenly, it seemed like the right time.

Sam suggested gentle guidelines. I would be completely in charge and we could sort things into categories: clothes I wanted to give to someone in particular (almost new snowmobile pants, for example), things no one would want (ratty t-shirts and old underwear), things I might keep for my own use (a down vest for staying warm in a drafty house on winter evenings), clothes I would just give away, and—most important—things I couldn't yet decide about. There was no pressure and Sam offered no opinions; he just took what I gave him, folding things into boxes at my direction—and returning any "I can't decide" items to the closet or the dresser.

It was a simple task, but I could not have done it alone, and had not wanted to do it sooner. Even after seven months, my hands shook sometimes during the process—but I felt good about it when we were done. We ended up with big boxes for a yard sale, for Goodwill, for a church that helps the job-seeking poor "dress for success," and for the trash. Sam took a barely used L. L. Bean barn coat for himself and the snowmobile pants for my nephew in snowy Rochester, NY. Several chamois shirts and the down vest, good for cold nights and yard work, stayed in my closet...along with the old green bathrobe, its secret scent hidden deep in the pocket.

Months went by. And then years.

The bathrobe frequently fell off its hook, landing in a heap on top of shoes or laundry basket or the closet floor. Darn you, I thought; but always, I picked it up and slung it back on the hook. Once in a while, I still reached into the pocket, to breathe again the faint and fading smell.

All my life, I've been a keeper of things; not a hoarder—I do throw things away—but certainly a pack rat. I keep things for different reasons. I save fabric, small snippets as well as big hunks, for crafts or quilts or spontaneous sewing projects with the grandchildren. Fabric holds memories: My biggest and most ambitious quilt, pieced over decades, is a fabric scrapbook of my wardrobe and experiences, from middle school to marriage.

I save the written word: letters and special cards and journals. To come upon Tracy's handwriting, or my dad's scrawl, or my two grandmothers' distinctive cursive styles, is to revisit our past togetherness, if just for a moment. I never had a chance to know my father's father, but reading his exuberant college-boy reflections on autumn in New England, carefully recorded with a fountain pen in a tiny pocket notebook, I find we are kindred spirits.

I save books. Who can get rid of a book once loved?

I save spices and baking supplies, because they are expensive, I don't use them quickly, and I am thrifty by nature. I have occasionally been stunned to discover particularly well-aged products in my cupboard: a box of cornstarch with a "use-by" date of 1987 that apparently moved with me three times; dried mustard in a tin not seen on grocery store shelves in decades. When I find such extremes, I do toss things. (Not a hoarder; just cheap.)

My packrat tendencies, combined with an early interest in family history, made me the Hamlin family archivist at a young age. In my teens, I became intrigued by the characters and story lines of my ancestors. Listening to parents, grandparents, great-aunts and distant cousins, my "keeper" instincts kicked in. Soon I had a collection of clippings, photos, letters, even a few cocktail napkins with notes hastily scribbled at family gatherings whenever someone mentioned something interesting from the past.

Years ago, I compiled much of that material into annotated genealogy posters for my family and began thinking it would fun to study the past through the real lives of those whose experiences combined to produce me. I kept collecting, taking every opportunity to ask relatives about their own early lives or stories they'd heard from their elders.

Somewhere along the way, curiosity about the past expanded to include anticipation of the future: As my parents found themselves attending more and more funerals, they began developing ideas about their own eventual memorials. Since I was the keeper of family history, they shared those thoughts with me; and thus was born the "Fabulous Funeral File." Bits of poetry, hymn titles, favorite music, meaningful scriptures, things they liked and things they definitely disliked—all came to me with the merry directive, "Put this in the Fabulous Funeral File!"

The whole family got into the habit of talking about what made a farewell celebration meaningful, or not. These conversations were never morose or glum; they were, instead, a quite congenial way of preparing to let go. And it helped me, a little, when the time came.

Although I never expected Tracy to die, I had always assumed I would outlive him. I had drafted his obituary once already and often thought about music I would want at a farewell. And then there were the seven weeks he lay in intensive care; the possibility of death was with us all the time. But possibility is not preparation. Neither is a funeral file.

There is no preparation for losing the love of your life. And when it happens, the last thing you want to do is let go.

Early on the morning of August 30, 2004, the day Tracy would die though I didn't know it yet, I rose early from fitful sleep and wrote: "I've been awake for—how long? I can't sleep. I tried to pray, but I can't seem to do that either—all I could think of was that hymn, 'Breathe on me, breath of God.' I try to remember Tracy's voice. What if I forget everything? I'm so sad. I can't imagine life without him being part of it."

What if I forget everything?

Later that day, after making the awful decision to disconnect the breathing apparatus, I stood at his bedside and held his hand for the few minutes it took (not hours or days, as the doctor had cautioned) for Tracy's spirit to leave his body. It left through his mouth, I thought—just as the 14th century woodcuts show in the medieval *Ars Moriendi*, the art of dying. It left when Tracy, eyes wide and looking somewhere beyond all of us, lifted his arms (he who hadn't been able to lift his arms for weeks) and silently mouthed the unmistakable words, "Mom, Mom."

"I held his hand the whole time," I wrote in my journal, late that night. "I told him not to be afraid, told him how much I loved him, told him to come back often to visit. I didn't want to let go. I wanted to hold his hand forever."

What if I forget? I want to hold on forever.

In the weeks and months that followed, the fear of forgetting, sometimes approaching panic, and the need to hold on washed over me often, overwhelming me with no warning.

Like the day I cleaned the medicine cabinet.

Pills and prescriptions had been a constant in Tracy's and my life together. First there was insulin, and with it all the needles, alcohol swabs and blood-sugar test strips that accompanied life with diabetes. Then, after the first kidney transplant, came the added regimen of medications to suppress the immune system, and more to protect against the side effects of immune suppression. From then on, "meds" were the bookends of our daily life.

In sickness and in health, Tracy sat at our kitchen table, morning and evening, counting out pills, checking them off in an 8 ½ x 11 notebook which was the only way he could be sure he remembered them all. Some were huge horse tablets; others were tiny and still had to be cut in half. With a cold or any infection, more pills joined the list. At the end, he was taking almost 20 pills, twice a day.

Several days after the funeral, my mother offered to help me clean out the "medicine cabinet," two deep closet shelves dedicated to medical paraphernalia. Good idea, I said. Tracy and I had been meaning to clean out the old meds for months.

In the midst of filling a 30-gallon bag with pills, tonics, creams, ointments, salves and syrups—some of them four, five, even six years outdated—I suddenly burst into tears. Who knew that throwing away old medicine could be so emotional? I sobbed on my mother's shoulder.

I had never before thought of Tracy's meds as anything but a necessary annoyance. It was a pain in the neck trying to remember to call in prescription refills, pick them up from the pharmacy, deal with the insurance company every month, remind Tracy to take them, urge him to hurry up when we were behind schedule in the morning. Modern medicine was a miracle, sure. But daily meds? They were a drag.

So I was not prepared for the grief that hit me as I stood tossing old pill bottles into a gaping plastic bag. But after fourteen years keeping track of medicine with Tracy every day, I felt like I was throwing away pieces of our marriage.

Letting go of the meds, and all they stood for, was hard, indeed.

The "medicine cabinet" became a linen closet. Life went on. Slowly, I felt my way through the emotional minefield of life without Tracy. What to keep? What to let go? How to remember?

What if I forget?

The spring after Tracy's death (when I still choked on the word, death), I decided to move ahead with a renovation of our family room, something Tracy and I had discussed for a long while. At first I tried to ask all the questions he would have asked and make the choices I thought he would have made. Gradually, though, I began to find my own voice in my discussions with the contractor. When the project was done—a complete make-over—I was thrilled with the results.

Ah, I thought, I'm better. I'm getting through this.

Hah.

Silly me.

Redoing that room was an important step for me, something I had never done before and thoroughly enjoyed. But it was also a way of holding onto life with Tracy, fulfilling by myself a dream we never quite got around to handling together.

Dealing with the back garage was something else entirely.

The "back garage," a separate building behind our house, was Tracy's domain, filled with his life and his passions: tool chests and workbenches, hunting and fishing equipment, shotgun shell re-loading supplies, auto repair materials, plumbing basics, and all the machines he used with such skill to build anything from a hydraulic drilling machine to an Adirondack chair to a saddle rack. My things—gardening tools and some riding tack—fit into one small corner.

Tracy was meticulous about his garage. He had installed a beautiful pine ceiling and bright new lights, and insulated two walls in preparation for making it a year-round workshop. He kept the space well-organized and very clean most of the time; but he had neglected it in the months leading up to the second kidney transplant, when he had so few days of feeling well. And shortly before the transplant, when he acquired more tools and equipment from his dad's estate, he deposited them randomly on any open spaces. It was uncharacteristic for him to accept such chaos, but he would rearrange everything later, he had said; he would do it after the transplant, when he felt well...

I knew the garage needed cleaning out. It was filled with items and equipment I could not identify, let alone put to any use. But each time I lifted the big garage door, stepped inside and tried to think of what to do or how to do it, I lasted no more than five minutes before feeling physically ill.

Get rid of his things? How can I do this?

I couldn't. The prospect of cleaning out the back garage literally made me sick.

So each time I closed the door, walked away and justified my decision: "Someday I'll learn how to use all of this stuff," I said.

It took six years for me to admit that I was never going to become a woodworker or a machinist or a handyman, nor even a handywoman. Though I was well out of the lonesome valley, the tools and machines, now covered in a thick layer of dust, could still make my stomach do flips. But I had just turned 60. I didn't have enough time for the writing, reading, riding, sewing and kayaking I already wanted to do. If and when I had more time, I wasn't likely to start learning to use heavy equipment. And though I love the outdoors, I wasn't ever going to become the kind of outdoorsman Tracy had been. I knew it was time.

When at last I began hauling things out of the back garage, on a beautiful summer day not long after what would have been our twentieth anniversary, I discovered I owned seventeen fishing rods. I was prepared to fish in any circumstance, winter or summer. The problem, though I hated to say so, was that I didn't like fishing.

I had never liked fishing.

I loved watching Tracy fish, watching him teach our grandson to fish, watching the delight with which he handled every lure in his cavernous tackle box: "What self-respecting bass could say no to this hula-popper?" I loved the eternal optimism with which he baited every hook and cast it out from shore or boat. I loved eating the fish after he'd cooked it. I loved that fishing was part of our outdoor vacations.

But I took a book with me in the boat. I didn't like to fish.

And I had seventeen fishing rods.

Some letting go was in order.

My brother-in-law, Glen, an avid fisherman like Tracy, helped me sort through the rods and reels.

The first step was the easiest: I admitted that ice fishing was definitely not in my future. I remembered vividly the dinner Tracy made for me of beer-battered blue gills caught on a Michigan lake one wickedly cold winter day before we were married: how surprised I was that I liked them, loved them in fact; how they melted in my mouth; how I hoped he would go ice fishing often and catch many more blue gills. And how glad I was that I was not the one who had to sit on the ice by a hole, waiting for the fish to swim beneath me and take my bait.

The ice fishing equipment would go to my nephew. I hoped he would love it and invite me for dinner.

Glen helped me identify the uses and conditions of the rest of the rods. We picked out three I might someday use with my grandchildren during the summer; I would keep those. The rest went with him, to be used, I hoped, with as much pleasure as Tracy had had from them.

Another weekend, a nephew came and helped rid me of an entire truckload of equipment and hardware I would never use. We laughed a lot that day. When he drove the truck away (looking, I had to admit, like a junk dealer), I gazed at my newly spacious garage and began imagining how I might use it.

Why was it so hard to get to this point? I wondered.

I had no answer then, and I have none now. If circumstances had forced me, if I had needed to sell the house for example, I surely could, and would, have tackled the garage sooner. But I love my house—and it is "my" house now, not "ours"—and I don't know when I might choose to leave it. I'm glad I was able to hold onto Tracy's beloved workshop until I could separate myself from it with a smile.

I'll never let go of the memories: Tracy opening his tackle box with a grin, loading shotgun shells at his reloading bench with Zen-like satisfaction, using his hand tools and his power saws with focused precision and creativity. Those images will be part of me forever. I know now I won't forget.

And who knows: maybe I will take the grandkids fishing someday. I bought a book called "Fishing for Kids" so I can learn if I need to. For now, I'm happy to work on setting up a potting shed for spring gardening, getting racks for my kayaks, organizing a summer craft bench.

About six months after the great garage clean-up, I decided I also had too much "stuff" inside my house. The house felt crowded and cramped, every room packed to the gills. I was drowning in excess paper and clothing and knick knacks and toys for the grandchildren and refrigerator magnets. I had to start getting rid of things.

You can do this, I told myself, tossing unread issues of The New Yorker into a pile for recycling. You can do this, I said again, giving myself permission to throw out old picture frames and send still-good but unworn-for-years shirts and skirts to a community center.

I gazed, finally, at the far end of the closet.

You can do this...

I took the green bathrobe from its hook. I pulled the handkerchief from its pocket, held it to my face and breathed in deeply. It smelled like old clothing. Nothing more.

Pausing for a moment, I remembered Tracy in that bathrobe: drinking coffee at our kitchen table, unwrapping presents on Christmas morning, walking the halls of various hospitals and getting well each time until he couldn't. Precious memories, all of them, and all firmly anchored in the treasure box of my heart.

I won't forget. Not a chance.

I folded the bathrobe and placed it gently on the give-away pile.

It took six-and-a-half years, but I let it go.

Going Places

Tracy and I had always loved going places. Mostly, we didn't go far; we just climbed into the Jeep and felt our way through the rural landscape of southeast Michigan or northwest Ohio with a compass, a thermos of coffee and an afternoon to kill. Sometimes, we'd park on the side of the road and take off on foot for a closer look at a promising bit of pheasant habitat. I felt like Daniel Boone's wife on those excursions—and I was always game for going.

Sometimes we went further afield: Chicago, Las Vegas, New England, the Upper Peninsula of Michigan.

Often, in our last few years, we never left home at all, exploring the world—real and imagined—with Robinson Crusoe, Long John Silver and Harry Potter. We took turns reading aloud.

A few times, we had the good fortune to visit truly exotic places, as far away as Korea and Taiwan.

Two years before we were married, when we still lived a three-hour drive apart, we decided to rendezvous in Greece. Tracy was heading to Europe for an extended business trip. I had signed up for a study-tour of ancient archeological sites. Why not meet in Athens at the end of our individual journeys? Of course, this was before email and internet, before cell phones and texting, so after departing on different days from airports in separate states, we would be completely out of touch for three weeks before meeting up. What if something went wrong? What if we couldn't find each other?

I felt like a character in a romantic thriller as I made my way through the streets of Athens toward the designated hotel at three o'clock on the appointed afternoon.

The hotel was a spectacular place, worthy of a James Bond novel. Standing on the marble floor beneath the high ceiling of the vast and sparkling lobby, I looked around nervously, scanning the crowd of dark-suited businessmen and high-heeled fashionistas and travelers speaking many languages, until...*yes!* Our eyes and smiles met. We'd made it. After a day at the Parthenon, Tracy and I flew to the Greek island of Crete, rented a car and spent the next five days wandering at will. Rita, the desk clerk at the first hotel we found, guessed we were on our honeymoon. We smiled and did not say no.

We loved visiting all those places. But it was never the destination that mattered. It was the exploring. And the togetherness.

"It doesn't really matter where we go," Tracy said once. "We could have a good time in Jasper," a tiny dot on the Michigan map, barely more than an intersection near the Ohio border.

A year after Tracy's death, and seventeen years after our romantic adventure in Greece, I joined my parents and siblings in Tortola, in the British Virgin Islands, for a clan vacation funded in part by the sale, and surprising value, of a piece of sculpture that stood unnoticed for years in the shadows of my grandmother's apartment. We toasted her memory often during a week of sun and daily snorkeling in the gem-like waters of the Caribbean.

Floating on the warm sea and swimming among the crazily colorful fishes magnified the unfamiliar sense of freedom I felt as that week went on: For the first time in many years, I was not responsible for anyone but myself.

I had never thought of loving and caring about Tracy as a burden or a restriction; but on our travels, and in our daily life, I was always on alert, trying to anticipate problems, mitigate difficulties in advance, ensure a good time for both of us. Tracy and I would not have taken this kind of Caribbean trip, at least not in his later years; much as he would have loved the adventure, neither his swim leg nor his stamina could have handled the long days of beach walking and deep-water snorkeling.

Now, as I kicked my leisurely way among reefs, into salt-water caves and over shipwrecks, each day swimming from a different beach or cove, I was buoyed by an unexpected ease and delight, an openness to unfettered exploration.

That trip might have been the beginning of a new chapter of going places, but back in Michigan, life was moving in a different direction. So instead, when I returned home, my focus realigned itself toward loving and encouraging and supporting the children and grandchildren whose lives were entering various sorts of rocky times.

Years went by.

I still went places, of course, and joyously, too; but not so much to explore as to renew and revitalize: I continued Tracy's and my tradition of taking kids and grandchildren to northern Michigan for a week each summer, a boisterous annual reaffirmation of our ties as family. I visited parents and siblings as often as possible on the east coast, especially cherishing the time with my father before his death and with my mother as she felt her way into the unfamiliar world of widowhood. I joined students on a service trip to the mountains of Jamaica and accompanied alumni to the hill towns of Tuscany.

I loved those travels and am grateful for every opportunity; but I did not again experience that exhilarating sense of boundless possibility that washed over me on the waters of Tortola. Not for a long time.

With the seventh anniversary of Tracy's death approaching, however, I once more embraced the freedom of wide-open exploration. In a "light bulb" moment of inspiration, I signed onto an adventure trip to Mongolia, a two-week horse trek among the nomads for a small group of fifteen people. I knew no one. I knew the diet would revolve around mutton, one of my least favorite foods. I knew there would be outhouses and no running water. I knew I would sleep in a tent with a sleeping bag. And I could not wait to go.

On the thireen-hour flight from Chicago to Beijing, I found a spot at the back of the plane where I could lean into a wide window-well, rest on my elbows, and gaze straight down as we flew across the top of the world, in sunlight the whole way. I marveled at the wilderness of northern Canada: lakes, lakes and more lakes in intricate jigsaw shapes cut into a vast sea of forest green. Later, I watched the Arctic spread out below, a rough carpet of white with great long cracks that traveled a jagged route across the ice to open ocean. Still later, I stared down onto barren mountains that looked like they had been carved by an artless giant, scratching lethal fingernails angrily into the earth. A spiderweb of rivers wriggled through the forbidding terrain like cracked grey grout.

"Where are we?" I wondered. "Northern China? Siberia? My geography is terrible..." I vowed to spend more time with the spinning globe on my desk when I got back home.

Then we were lower. Hints of green appeared on the mountain slopes. Lower still, vast watery stretches glittered in the sun like giant rice paddies.

The earth is an incredible place, I thought, more than once.

Eventually, I determined we probably flew over Mongolia to reach Beijing. After a five hour layover, wandering among airport pagodas and staring out at the famous Beijing smog, I boarded another plane for the several-hour flight back north and west to Ulaanbaator, the capital and only real city in Mongolia. By now, night was catching up; we landed in darkness and I wondered how far the airport was from the city. Not far, it turned out; but this was not like a night arrival in any city in the U.S. Except for the runway lights, it was pitch black.

Stepping out of the plane, I was met by a wonderful gust of fresh cold air. I like this place already, I thought, breathing deeply in the chilly darkness.

My journey to Mongolia had begun in Michigan at 6:30 a.m. June 29 when I left my house for the Detroit airport; it was 11:30 p.m. June 30 when I arrived in Ulaanbaator. Even accounting for the thirteen-hour time difference, it was a long haul. But already, I was overwhelmed, full-up with the richness of what I had seen and taken in. And the trip I'd signed on for had not yet even begun.

I spent the next two weeks with an energetic and congenial roommate and a posse of like-minded traveling companions, eagerly embracing each new experience. After two days in U.B.— as Ulaanbator was commonly called—we packed into a twenty-passenger mini-bus and headed south and west to the Hrangay Mountains. Bouncing over dirt roads and gravel plains, washed out riverbeds and uneven pastures, with only occasional stretches of pavement, we made our way to Lapis Sky camp on the Tamir River, our headquarters for the remainder of our stay.

With us and our luggage, the bus was too heavy for the last leg of the journey, up and over a steep and craggy pass (no road here) into the river valley; so the bus and the baggage went one way while we walked another way for the last mile into camp. Our shortcut, over an even rougher pass, revealed a settlement of "gers," the round moveable yurts that have been home to the nomads of Mongolia for centuries, on the green plain far below. Picking my way through the loose rocks down to the valley floor, I never guessed how well I would come to know that pass, riding my sturdy horse, Khase, over and back many times.

Many things had drawn me to Mongolia: the ancient nomadic culture, the fascinating and unfamiliar history, the remote rugged landscape. I loved the idea of venturing to a place still so unknown, almost a true frontier. But more than anything, it was the horses that captured my imagination, from the moment I opened the travel brochure on my kitchen table one winter evening, decompressing from a day's work with a glass of wine and the day's mail. With one glance at the picture of brightly clad riders on the wide-open steppe, I was hooked.

As it turned out, horses were a pretty good reason to go; because in Mongolia, even today, horses are part of almost everything.

Genghis Khan's warriors successfully conquered a large part of the known world in the 13th century because of their leader's innovative thinking—and because of the strength and stamina of Mongolia's sturdy mountain horses. Eight centuries later, for the nomad families in central Mongolia, survival still depends on hard work, planning, weather, luck...and the strength and stamina of their horses.

When today's nomads move from winter to summer camps, they pack up satellite dishes and solar panels (for the computer and the television) along with traditional wood-burning stoves and collapsible felt-covered gers. But they still rely on horses (sometimes with an occasional motorcycle) to manage their herds of goats, sheep, yaks and more horses; and to travel across the largely empty landscape, visit distant neighbors, and gallop for glory in the annual Naadam festival races. Nomad children grow up helping with the animals and learn to ride at a young age; we saw children of eight or nine on horseback, herding sheep miles from the family ger. And the Naadam jockeys—who race bareback across the steppe for twelve miles or more—are always young girls and boys; the riders may compete starting at age five but must "retire" when they reach fourteen.

Horses show up almost everywhere in Mongolia. Children and adults ride casually through small-town marketplaces. Loose horses graze next to the roads and wander at will to the other side, even crossing the highways leading into and away from Ulaanbaator. All drivers brake for horses. In downtown U.B., famous for its honking traffic jams, cars and trucks sometimes share the road with four-legged transport: On a main thoroughfare near Sukhbaatar Square, not far from the upscale Louis Vuitton store, I watched shiny new sedans zoom past a man on horseback, moving at an easy trot and leading a second horse ridden by a woman; behind both riders and horses, a lively foal followed freely, no lead rope at all. No one was fazed.

In another tip-of-the-hat to the importance of horses in Mongolia's past (and perhaps to its growing tourist trade), the "walk/don't-walk" lights at intersections in central U.B. feature, instead of a red hand or a green walking man, a red standing horse and a green trotting horse. Tacky? Tasteful? I wasn't sure; but I loved it.

What really surprised me was hearing horses in the traditional music of Mongolia. In a concert-hall in U.B., before heading out to our own horseback adventure, we first encountered the sounds of traditional throat singing and the playing of the morin khuur, or horsehead fiddle. Two weeks later, we heard the music again; this time we were up close to the performers, seated on logs and benches around a camp fire in the Hrangay Mountains.

Throat singing, called khoomii, is a guttural sound unlike anything that comes out of American mouths. The Mongolian language also includes this guttural vocalization, making it extremely difficult for western speakers; I pride myself on being good at languages, but I never conquered even a recognizable "thank you." (My only reliable word in Mongolian was "cho." Uttered with gruff depth, cho is the universal word for "go" for riders on horseback, the Mongolian equivalent of "giddy-up.")

Khoomii is a rare gift, even among Mongolians; and khoomii singers are greatly respected. The best of them can produce an otherworldly duet of deep almost subterranean notes with a thin birdlike melody floating above it. That's right: two notes at once—one very high, one incredibly low—coming from one voice. Heard in the U.B. concert hall, the sound was eerie, magical. Heard the second time, outdoors in the mountains, khoomii evoked the vast loneliness of warriors, or nomads, alone with their horses under Mongolia's eternal blue sky or star-studded night universe.

The morin khuur is a two-stringed cello-like instrument with a trapezoidal sound box and a long neck that curves at its top into the beautifully carved head of a horse. In the hands of a master, the two flat strings of the morin khuur are enough to produce complicated European classics as well as the distinctive music of Mongolia. On our last night at Lapis Sky camp, as twilight dimmed into darkness around the bright bonfire, a young musician, resplendent in an embroidered white robe and white boots with the traditional upturned toes, sat to play for us. First, he played Mozart, perhaps just to show that he, and his instrument, could do it. And without question, he could do it. Then, he began playing the hypnotic compositions of his homeland. And running through that haunting music was the unmistakable rhythm of hoof beats across the steppe.

I had heard those rhythms before in U.B. But now, after many days on horseback, I recognized them in a deeper way. I heard and felt each gait...

The easy plod of horses wandering freely through camp one early morning before most people were awake—or the delicate cadence of a single horse and rider casually exploring this vast land.

The famous running trot that carried Genghis Khan's armies 50 miles and more in a day—and took me down a miles-long valley all by myself, no other riders in sight, when I was slower than the fastest in our group, but faster than the slowest.

The all-out gallop of warriors in attack. Or whole herds of horses startled into a dead run. Or me on Khase, with our other top riders and the Mongolian horsemen, all retracing a two-day ride in just four hours. Thunderhoofing, our leader called it, as we pushed fast and hard for home through the cowboy landscape. Thrilling beyond belief, I called it.

All of that was there in the proud music of the morin khuur.

Yes, in Mongolia, the spirit of the horse was everywhere. And one day, I found it in religion.

At the Buddhist monastery of Erdene Zhu, on the grassy plains of Kharkhorin, I and my fellow-travelers sat cross-legged on the floor facing the head lama, who also sat cross-legged, his burgundy robe over one shoulder. With the help of our interpreter, the lama spoke about Mongolian Buddhism and its miraculous survival despite ninety years of Communist efforts to destroy religion.

I discovered quickly that I was out of practice at sitting cross-legged. (How long had it been? I had no idea.) I twisted and fidgeted. My knees and hips ached as the lama explained how Mongolians had buried some of their Buddhist relics and secretly maintained their beliefs through the Soviet era. As uncomfortable as I was, though, I knew I was right where I belonged when the lama began speaking about *hiimor*, the spirit of the "wind horse," a concept unique to Mongolian Buddhism.

Hiimor is a natural force that breathes energy into an individual's life, the lama explained. The horse is in tune with his surroundings, he said: eating when he is hungry, running when he wants, spirited and independent, comfortable wherever he is.

So, too, *hiimor,* the wind horse, inspires and empowers one's soul, the lama said. *Hiimor* brings passion to one's existence, and puts one right with the world.

"I am so in the right place," I thought.

Returning from this vast and beautiful country where I fulfilled—and exceeded—every horseback riding dream of my tomboy childhood, I found myself thrilled by the beat of my own hiimor.

Through Tracy's illness and after his death, the hymn that meant the most to me was this: "Breathe on me, breath of God. Fill me with life anew." Breath like wind. Wind like breathing.

The God of us all filled me with new life in Mongolia, breathing on me, in me, around me. My wind horse came alive in the Hrangay Mountains and runs with me still.

"Cho!" I called out to my Mongolian mountain horse, urging him on to next ridge, the next long gallop, the next nomad encampment or our own home ger.

"Cho!" I call to my wind horse.

This is not a call to break away from family ties, not a tossing off of responsibilities or concern for others. It is a declaration of wholeness, of independence; a strengthening of my core and my commitments—to love, to live, to learn and grow, to explore. Far away? Perhaps. Or maybe just around the corner.

"Cho. *Cho!*"

And louder now: "Cho! Go!"

"Take me to the next place! I am ready."

After Words

Ours was not a Hallmark love story.

Over the years many friends and relatives commented on the bond Tracy and I shared, and how much we enjoyed being together. I don't argue with that; I cherish every moment we had. But our delights were hard won, and I would not counsel anyone to follow the path we chose to follow—or at least chose not to abandon. The chances of it all working out, as it did eventually for us, are very small.

Tracy and I had known each other seven-and-a-half years by the time we married. Those were not easy years. There were tears, for us and for others. There was sadness, confusion, guilt, and anger; and there were many tough choices. Three times we ended it. Finally, I moved to another state. Tracy ended a twenty-one-year marriage. We both sought counseling. I wouldn't recommend this route to anyone. But I wouldn't change it. And I'll never regret it. It's who I am now.

No, Tracy and I were not perfect.

But we were lucky. Very lucky.

We had the good fortune to meet each other at a time in our lives when we both had the capacity to appreciate each other's differences. Had we met when we were younger, we might never have noticed each other, never given friendship a thought. Despite the obvious unlucky aspect of our situation—that he was married when we met—we were, nonetheless, lucky that circumstances put us in the same place at the same time for long enough that we had a chance to talk and to get that first taste of delight in each other's company. The first taste was all it took; that spurred us to look for more.

And then, there is the bigger and more amazing piece of luck: that we were able to respond and grow together in ways we could not have anticipated. We were this lucky: We each became better, fuller, different people in response to the other. When I talk with my daughters now about Tracy—and we almost always talk about him at some point when we're together—the funny or bittersweet stories they tell from their childhoods, from the years "before me," often paint a picture of a different man than the one I knew.

We were lucky in another way, also. Two people falling in love don't think about this kind of luck, but it might be the most important in the long run: Our families welcomed the partners we chose.

My parents and siblings and extended family all anguished with me over the heartaches of my tangled seven-year friendship with Tracy before we married; then embraced him, and our daughters and grandchildren, as fully as any in-laws could.

Tracy's family had every reason to reject or resent me as a home-wrecker, or worse. But they didn't. His mother and father, sister and brother, and a whole clan of cousins and shirt-tail relations, opened their collective arms, inviting me in as the newest "Church lady."

His children—Cindy, Sarah and Michelle—allowed me into their lives, not as "mom" but as Jennifer. So now they are my daughters, too, still and forever.

Most remarkable of all, and most lucky for Tracy and me, once he had left his first marriage—once it was clear that union was definitely over—his ex-wife never begrudged me my relationship with the girls, nor sought to poison their relationship with their father. She never prevented the girls from spending time with us or sabotaged our efforts at building a new kind of family. Eventually, Judy and her second husband and Tracy and I became a sort of parental team, standing up together as a foursome at high school sports banquets and honors nights, birthday parties, graduations and weddings. These family ties, unusual as they may be, have endured even beyond Tracy's death. I and my "co-grandparents" continue to share concerns and support for our children and our children's children. How lucky is that?

"We were so lucky," I wrote to Tracy in my journal, two months after his death. We were "two independent people so happy to have found, fought for, and chosen each other. We chose each other often, again and again, morning after morning."

Not a Hallmark story, but I will forever be grateful.

A good friend of mine, a writer and English professor at Siena Heights who had been one of Tracy's teachers, wrote a poem that she read at Tracy's funeral:

A Valediction

Lying in solemnity
On the altar of his bed,
Tracy,
Pinioned and perplexed,
Waited for the light.
When it arrived,
Blazing with the truth
That love is stronger than death,
His spirit slipped through the bars of his fears

And soared
Swiftly and surely as an engineer's tool
Into the waiting mercies
Of his God.

Patricia Schnapp, RSM

After the funeral, I pinned that poem to my bulletin board at work, along with a small prayer card given to me by an Adrian Dominican Sister quoting Luke 23:43: "This day you will be with me in paradise." Nine years later, they remain on the board, buried somewhere beneath important phone numbers and to-do lists and new photos of friends and grandchildren. And somewhere at home, I have the other card, the one quoting Victor Hugo.

> *Love is stronger than death.*
> *You will be with me in paradise.*
> *To love another person is to see the face of God.*

Grief is different for each person, but those were the mantras that guided and reassured me on my long journey through love and loss and back into the light of life.

Tracy and I were in our early forties when we married, and I became a wife, a mother and a grandmother. Barely fourteen years later, I kissed him goodbye and held his hand as he left us. I wanted to hold his hand forever.

He is gone now, but I am still a mother, a grandmother, and now a great-grandmother. What greater gift could he have left me?

I still miss him—his smile, his humor and curiosity, his love, his staunch refusal to let illness define him. I will always miss him; I understand that now. But I no longer ache with missing. Somewhere along the way, missing moved into the background and made room for living. Now, in those moments of longing that still ambush me every once in a while, I can smile, accepting the memory—and the missing—as a gift.

In church, I sing all the hymns, even when the words remind me of Tracy. I don't dissolve when I hear "In the Garden:"

> I come to the garden alone,
> when the dew is still on the roses,
> and the voice I hear falling on my ear
> the son of God discloses.

Instead, I am happy remembering our last spring together, and the day I planted the new flower bed that Tracy had built for me along the side of the house. I was on my knees in the early morning sun, digging small holes in the dirt, gently positioning the seedlings, patting the dirt back down and dreaming of blossoms to come. I looked up to find that Tracy had made his careful way out to the garden, slowly, with a cane, to check in and see how I was doing.

> And he walks with me, and he talks with me,
> and he tells me I am his own.
> And the joys we share as we tarry there,
> none other has ever known.

I sing the words and smile, even though it is true, now, that I "come to the garden alone." I have made my peace with the facts of life. And death.

One afternoon during Tracy's long stay in intensive care that last summer, I stood by his bed, talking softly and stroking his hand, hoping he might wake up for a few moments. This was a non-responsive day. I hoped he could feel my presence; and that at some deep level he knew I was there and was comforted by my closeness.

Inside the cavernous room—large enough to accommodate multiple doctors plus any roll-in medical machinery that might be needed at a moment's notice—the lights were dimmed. Beyond the door, outside the glass wall, it was ultra-bright around the ICU nurses' station.

"Hi, honey. I'm right here," I said softly. "I hope you're having lovely dreams right now."

Around the bed, monitors blinked and clicked and whirred. For the moment, there was no annoying beeping—nothing was out of sync. But Tracy was far away in a place I couldn't reach.

"Don't you want to wake up and say hi?" I urged quietly, trying to will him into consciousness. I stroked his cheek and hoped I didn't sound like I was pleading. But I knew I was.

Voices. Then movement.

I looked up to see a herd of docs gathering by the door, outside the glass wall, interns in green scrubs, one fellow in a white coat with a clipboard, obviously in charge. It felt like hundreds of scenes from TV medical shows: doctors making their rounds in a teaching hospital.

"Can he even be 15?" I wondered about the astonishingly youthful head doctor. He was not one of "our" doctors, not one of the surgeons or any of the residents I'd been meeting with. I hadn't seen him before. He had the group's attention, and was gesturing with his hands as he spoke.

He's reviewing the case with the interns, I thought. I tried to listen.

"Now this guy..." His arm swept casually behind him toward the bed.

Rage erupted in my chest, and in my throat. Blood pounded in my ears.

'*This guy?*' I thought.

This guy? My husband—my miracle man? *This guy?*

I don't know what else he said. I didn't listen. All I knew right then was that I had to speak. I had to speak up for "this guy," for

Tracy. I left the bed and whispered to the nurse making entries in the notebook by the door.

"Who...is...this...doctor?" I hissed through clenched teeth.

"Oh," she said cheerily, "this is Dr. ___. He's one of our ICU doctors. You haven't met him? He's wonderful, let me introduce you." She turned and caught his attention.

"Dr. ____, this is Mrs. Church. The patient's wife."

He turned, surprised but respectful, and said hello. Then he waited. I guess he could see I had something on my mind.

"I just want you to know..."

I paused. What did I want him, all of them, to know?

"I just want you to know that my husband...Tracy...is a really smart man..."

I took a breath, and then the words tumbled out.

"He's a brilliant engineer. He designs and builds complex machines that are bigger than this room. He reads history and philosophy, and he writes short stories. He used to race motorcycles. He loves children, especially his grandchildren. And he trains dogs and loves to go bird hunting, and fishing. And he's very funny. If he could talk now...if he didn't have that tube down his throat... he would tell you a joke or make a funny comment about sports or the weather. He'd want to know how all these machines work. And he'd ask you about your family and your kids. He would say 'good morning' and shake your hand and thank you for trying to help him. He does that with doctors."

I could feel the tears dripping down my face to my chin. But I wasn't quite through.

"The other thing is, Tracy has an incredible will to live and if you give him even half a chance, he will fight his way back. And..."

I paused, thinking about what it all meant.

"And I just think it's important that you know that 'this guy,' this wonderful loving creative man—just like every other patient in here—is so much more than test results and symptoms and that big fat notebook.

"He's not just...a body in a bed."

I took a ragged breath and tried to exhale normally.

"Thank you," I said finally. There was no more to say.

Silence. It felt like a long time.

Then one intern reached out a hand: "I'm Dr. ____. Thank you." Then another and another. One by one, they each extended a hand, introduced themselves, and thanked...me. After a few moments, they moved on to the next patient.

In the weeks that followed, they would nod when our paths crossed. They couldn't know Tracy like I did, but I felt better. Maybe they knew something about me.

As months, and then years, went by after Tracy's death, I felt the need to speak up again; but this time I would write. I still wanted people to know Tracy. And I wanted to share the journey that he and I had taken together. I wanted to share the other journey, too— the one I had to travel alone, like so many others who have loved someone to, and beyond, the end.

"Just give us five years," I had said at the beginning. We got fourteen. It was not enough, of course. Nothing would be enough. My Mom and Dad got sixty-one years, but Mom wishes they'd had more. Still, the time we had was a gift beyond measure.

It's been more than nine years since I held Tracy's hand as he left this world for the next one, nine years since I began learning to make sense of a world without Tracy in it. I still miss him in private moments. I still say "hello" to him now and then, when I am surprised by a white sun. He will always be part of who I am, even as I go, and grow, in new and unexpected directions.

I have done well, people say: I have been strong. I have grieved but I have healed and moved forward. I have re-embraced life.

I think they are right; though I feel the same way Tracy and I once felt when people asked how we coped: What other choice is there, really?

Still, I am amazed. I would not believe he could be gone so long, except for the solid evidence all around me: the births and the birthdays, weddings and divorces, the growing grandchildren—many now taller than I am, the home improvements, even the funerals and farewells.

A song at our wedding went, "Even on a cold gray morning, we can see the sunlight shine." That was always true for us. Through all the obstacles and medical challenges Tracy faced, we laughed, loved and cherished each day.

A song at his funeral went, "Love changes everything. Nothing in the world will ever be the same." That, too, is true. I carry within me the life-changing gift of his love. And each day I try to reflect that love, sharing it with the daughters and grandchildren he brought into my life, and lighting my way to new dreams, new pathways and possibilities.

"Don't be surprised if I hug you to death," he said, the last time he could say anything to me. It was a hug—a love—to death, through death, and back to life. To learning and growing again. To living on with an open heart.

There is, still, so much to live for.

L'chaim! Cho!

After Words

Notes & Acknowledgements

Acknowledgements

Grateful thanks go, first and foremost, to everyone in my Hamlin and Church families, without whom the journey described here would have been so much sadder and more difficult. My parents, Norman and Barbara Hamlin, were, as they always had been (and as Mother still is), my strongest supporters and greatest fans. My siblings and in-laws—Becky and Bob Pine and Sam and Eve Hamlin in the East; Cristal and Glennis Milner and Dexter and Linda Church in Michigan (and now Utah)—have been friends, confidantes, counselors, hand-holders, and reliable sources of fun, even in hard times. My daughters and their families have given me reasons to laugh, love, live, sometimes cry, and always look forward to the next day. Nieces and nephews, on both Tracy's and my side, have been wonderful in many ways, sharing frequent practical support and making me feel like a very special Aunt Jennifer (or Janie). Aunts, uncles and cousins were unfailingly supportive. I am grateful to you all, and to many more in the pantheon of extended relations. No one could ask for a better family.

Many people provided creative encouragement through the writing process. Sister Pat Schnapp, RSM, was my writing buddy and advisor from start to finish. Mom was always willing to listen to my latest "piece" over the phone, offer practical feedback, and share her own work as well; she is an inspiration. My Siena Heights alumni pen pal, children's book writer Ann Tompert, never let me forget to get back to writing, to keep on writing—and then to do something with what I wrote. My good friends Kathie Duckworth and Connie Aichele encouraged my writing as we all explored new creative outlets and committed ourselves to checking in annually with results. My long-time friend, artist-turned-writer Mary Beath, provided outstanding feedback and fruitful advice at a critical point in the development of the manuscript. Further on, Alexander Weinstein and Ann Kimmage helped nudge me into some of the hard stuff. I am grateful to all my early readers for their interest and helpful suggestions as I revised the draft; in addition to those already mentioned, I thank Paula Domitio, Janice Harris, Dr. Sue Idczak, Pat and Elaine Sheehan, Mary Pinkerton, Cynthia Garrells, Karen Fraker, Mary Weeber, Karen Glaser, and my siblings, Becky and Sam. John MacNaughton generously guided me through uncharted territory as my design and production mentor.

Epworth United Methodist Church in Toledo, Ohio, provided a spiritual home before, through and beyond grief. For two decades, Epworth members, musicians and ministers have helped me (and Tracy, earlier) make sense of living.

Special thanks to Ken Streitenberger for compassionate hospital ministry and invariably helpful preaching from the pulpit through some of the darkest times.

Finally, I will be forever grateful to the doctors, nurses and medical staff who treated Tracy, and me, with dignity, diligence and compassion. These include:

- the doctors and nurses of Nephrology Associates of Northwest Ohio, especially Drs. Gurdeep Singh, Brian Savage and Bikram Johar—you were Tracy's constant companions for 15 years;
- transplant surgeon Dr. Steven Selman and 1989 transplant coordinator Carolyn Wolfe at Medical College of Ohio Hospital;
- transplant surgeon Dr. Mitchell Henry and his colleagues at The Ohio State University Medical Center in 1998-99 and again in 2004; and the summer 2004 residents, especially Drs. Denny and Barrett;
- Shawn Milner, nurse extraordinaire, who oversaw Tracy's care on

so many visits to the Toledo Hospital emergency room—and made sure his uncle laughed whenever possible;

- many Toledo area specialists, including vascular surgeon Dr. Ralph Whalen, podiatrist Dr. John Lane, cardiothoracic surgeon Dr. Michael Moront, and orthopedic surgeons Dr. Robert Hartwig and Dr. Karl Beer; and the diligent professionals at Hanger Prosthetics & Orthotics;

- and the many other doctors, nurses, aides and associates, no doubt numbering in the hundreds, whose names I never learned, many of whom I never met, who played a part in the events described in the text, and many other incidents not mentioned in this book.

Note: Several medical facilities mentioned in this book have undergone name changes in recent years. In the text, I chose to use the names by which we knew them:

- The Medical College of Ohio Hospital, commonly known as MCO when Tracy was a kidney transplant recipient there in 1989, is now the University of Toledo Medical Center, UTMC.
- The Ohio State University Medical Center, also referred to in the text simply as OSU, has been renamed and is now the Wexner Medical Center at Ohio State University.

Timeline of Selected Medical Events *in Tracy's life*

February 24,1948	Tracy Church born, Hudson, Michigan.
December 1961	Diagnosed with juvenile diabetes.
December 1988	Begins kidney dialysis for the first time.
November 1989	Kidney transplant, MCO; last dialysis in Dec.
July 1990	Marries Jennifer in Maine.
August 1990	Below-the-knee amputation of right leg.
June 1998	Pancreas transplant, OSU.
September 1998	Heart catheterization.
October 1998	Pancreas rejection episode, OSU.
May 1999	Enteric conversion surgery, OSU.
November 2000	Colitis episode.
Spring/Summer 2001	Tracy supports Jennifer through breast cancer.
December 2001	Begins dialysis for the second time.
April 2002	First heart attack.
June 2002	Heart bypass surgery.
Spring 2003	First finger amputation and revision.
May 2003	Second heart attack; stent installed.
August 2003	Pacemaker/defibrillator installed.
Fall 2003	Second finger amputation.
Winter/Spring 2004	Third finger amputation and revision.
March 2004	Heart catheterization and stent revision.
June 2004	Cardiac ablation, Toledo.
June 2004	Kidney transplant #2, OSU.
July 2004	Pneumonia; admitted to Toledo Hospital.
July 2004	Transferred to OSU intensive care.
August 30, 2004	Farewell and Godspeed.

Good Grief

Good grief," says Charlie Brown, whenever something unexpected or surprising or problematic happens. Then we all chuckle, as the enigmatic comic strip character and his "Peanuts" friends muddle through whatever circumstance has befallen them.

It's a strange turn of phrase, really, "good grief." And as it is used most often, it refers not at all to grieving, but rather to mild surprise or disbelief. For Charlie Brown, it might be: "You mean my kite is caught in the tree again?" Or, "My outfielder missed that fly ball? Seriously?" He can hardly believe it. "Good grief."

Surprisingly, the grief that follows the loss of a loved one has some things in common with those scenarios. No matter how anticipated a death might be, the reality of loss is always unexpected, surprising and problematic. And there is certainly disbelief, although it exists hand-in-hand with cold hard reality.

Three weeks after my husband died, I joined a three-month grief support group that was titled, "Good Grief." The leader gently cautioned me that it was awfully soon after Tracy's death; and if, after we started, I felt it was too soon or I was too raw, it would be alright to step out of the group and wait for the next offering of the program.

But in fact, for me, it was the right time. I leaned heavily on that group and found myself eagerly awaiting each weekly gathering of fellow travelers who understood...everything. Some were several months past a death; some were years past a loss; but all needed to grieve and mourn in order to move on.

That was the first lesson I learned about grief. There is no universal timetable. It is not a one-size-fits-all experience. There is no prescribed path, no reliable calendar. Each person's grief is theirs and theirs alone. Each person follows a different route, backing and forthing on their own circuitous way to a new sense of normalcy.

But even though each person's experience of grief is different, there are things we can teach each other, feelings we can share, helpful strategies for negotiating a new and changed life. For anyone struggling with the loss of a loved one, I offer a few gentle suggestions—things that helped me, and have been helpful to others, too.

First is the importance of doing something. Anything. Even something as simple as making your bed or making breakfast. I've come to call this piece of advice: do the next thing.

The emotions of grief can be paralyzing. Getting through the day, or the night, can seem impossibly difficult. Focusing on one "next" thing, however mundane, then celebrating your own success in doing that thing, is a simple way to keep yourself going, no matter what your timetable or where you are on the journey.

Over time, the challenges will change. But again and again, in the grief groups I have been privileged to help shepherd, people come back to this simple mantra: Do the next thing. Just one thing. Then pat yourself on the back. Be proud of yourself. You did it.

Then look for the next thing.

A second suggestion has to do with that elusive "sense of normalcy." Immediately after a great loss, many of us turn to the structures that have always supported us. Maybe it's a pattern of behavior: morning coffee at the kitchen table. Or maybe it's the friends with whom we've always socialized. Perhaps it's the commitments we've always had to church or community. Whatever the specifics, most of us reach, at the beginning, for the reassurance of old familiar ways.

Then, sometimes, comes disappointment. The old familiar ways don't seem to work. Perhaps your friends are all couples, and now you're a fifth wheel. Maybe your prior commitments were shaped by your loved one's needs or interests. Maybe, as I found, your morning coffee was always flavored with laughter…and now there is silence. Discovering that the old "normal" is gone, along with the person you lost, is another layer of grief. Sometimes, like an onion, grief has many layers; and each new layer uncovered can make you cry.

So part of the journey is finding, or creating, a new normal. It can be a very sad process, and a difficult one, and—like so much about grief—it happens again and again. What will my new normal be for breakfast? For Saturday nights or Sunday afternoons? What about family birthdays? How on earth will I manage Christmas? It goes on and on. A great loss changes just about everything, so finding a new way to define normal—to build normal—to feel and be normal—is not a one-time endeavor. For a while anyway, it becomes a way of life.

Grief can be surprisingly complicated, too; as complicated as our own emotions and experiences. Fear, regret, guilt, relief, shame, anger, bitterness, abandonment: all of these may be part of grief, along with the more "expected" and "accepted" feelings of sadness, longing and loneliness. Sometimes friends and family have no tolerance for these complicated emotions; and sometimes we can barely admit them to ourselves, let alone to others. The appearance of such unexpected—and unsupported—emotions can add to the isolation that grievers sometimes feel. But emotions don't go away on their own. Finding someone willing to listen, or even just talking honestly with yourself, is a first step to letting go of that pain.

That leads to another hard truth.

Contrary to popular belief, time does not heal all wounds, at least not by itself. However grief manifests itself, and whatever feelings are involved, getting through it takes work. That is the deeper lesson implicit in "do the next thing." It takes effort to create a new normal, and it takes time. You aren't always in charge of the process, but you do have to be an active participant.

Focusing on the good things in your life is always helpful, though it is not as simple as "looking on the bright side." To be honest, there is no bright side to death and loss. But identifying even little things for which you are grateful—the appearance of the first crocus of spring, a bright red cardinal at your winter bird feeder, a call from a friend, a hot bowl of soup—and articulating your thanks for such things, whether in prayer or in a journal or just in your own mind, can help you get through the day. Making a list of things that make you smile, and then deliberately seeking out one such thing every day, can help you feel that you have some small degree of control over your life.

Many people who are grieving benefit from some kind of support group. I certainly looked forward to talking with other people who wanted to talk about the same things that concerned me—and most grievers find that friends eventually tire of your grief, or are embarrassed by it, or just don't know how to respond. The opportunity to share openly with people outside your normal social circle, and outside your family, can be very helpful. Support groups are very different, however; and I have met many people who tried several groups before finding the right fit.

Mild depression is not uncommon during times of grief, though it is never fun. Clinical depression, however, may call for more serious intervention; and suicidal thoughts at any time demand immediate help. If grief is causing you, or someone you know, to consider ending life, seek professional help through a hotline, a church, a therapist, a doctor— or a friend who can connect you to one of those sources of assistance. Neither families nor support groups are prepared or equipped to respond sufficiently to deep depression or suicidal manifestations of grief. Seek professional assistance.

For most people, grief ultimately will prove to be a manageable, if extended, experience. It will change your life, just as the loss you experienced changed your life. Grief may never be "over," never "done;" even many years later, it may catch you unawares now and then.

Eventually grief may prove to have enriched your life in some unexpected ways, though most of us would gladly trade the "enrichment" for the person we lost. As my mother once put it, "I'm doing well. I have a good life and I am happy. But I don't think I will ever enjoy life without Norman as much as I enjoyed it with him."

- Do the next thing.
- Create a new normal.
- Do the work; don't expect time to handle it if you don't play a part.
- Focus on good things and choose to smile when you can.
- Seek community.

Everyone's grief is their own. No one's experience of mourning will be exactly like anyone else's. But those are a few of the practical "to do" ideas that guided me, day by day, through the journey I have recalled in this book. I hope they will help others.

I, too, have a good life, and my days are happy. I will always be sorry that Tracy and I did not have more time together, but I am so glad we had the years we did have.

And I can't wait to see what life has in store.

Epilogue
Diabetes Today

This is a story about love, grief and faith; medical miracles, mortality and the joy of being alive. It is not a story about diabetes. But diabetes is a major player in the story, underlying and influencing just about everything else. And the story of diabetes itself is still being written, all around us.

One day, during that summer at the OSU Medical Center, I stood at Tracy's bedside. Elbows tight against my ribs, I clasped and unclasped my hands below my chin staring at Tracy's face, wishing, wondering. He had been unresponsive for several days.

"What if he had a stroke?" I thought suddenly. "Would I know?"

Once formulated in my mind, the question would not go away. The next time I saw a doctor, I had to ask.

"Is it possible he's had a stroke? Is there any way to know?"

The doctor looked dubious. "I don't think he's had a stroke," he said. Then: "The only way to tell for sure is with a CAT scan."

That was that. I knew the doctors were reluctant to move him for tests when he was so unstable. I didn't pursue it.

But when I came the next day, the doctor was back.

"He hasn't had a stroke," he reported. "We did a scan. There wasn't anything unusual in the brain. Just the normal diabetic changes you would expect."

Just the normal diabetic changes you would expect?

In the brain...?

Well, of course, I thought bitterly: Diabetes had already affected everything else—kidneys, veins, arteries, heart, eyes, feet, fingers. Why not the brain, too?

Diabetic changes in the brain. Who knew?

I remembered that incident several weeks after Tracy's death when my own doctor, trying to be sympathetic and supportive, described diabetes as a sort of "cancer of the whole body." Diabetes affects the blood and the blood feeds everything else. Eventually, you could "expect" diabetic changes everywhere.

Diabetes is a devastating disease which, over time, can damage every organ and every system in the human body. This is true, eventually, for both Type 1 and Type 2 diabetes. They are different diseases with the same deadly outcome, separate tributaries to the same mighty river of destruction. To ignore the disease is to be done in by it, in more ways than you can imagine.

Tracy lived a full life because he was adamant that he would lead a full life. He would not be defined by affliction. He wrestled with diabetes for most of his life; lost a leg because of it at 42. "But don't call me a diabetic or an amputee," he said. "Call me a person."

He hoped people would think of him, remember him, as an entrepreneur, an outdoorsman, a reader and writer, husband and father, son and brother, who just happened to face a few medical challenges in his life. He never mentioned medical problems in social conversation; never used health as an excuse to get out of doing his fair share. And as a result, many people in our circle of acquaintances never knew he had health problems. In that way, he defied diabetes.

But he lived with diabetes as long as he did because, at least in the twenty-one years that I knew him, he respected the disease, recognized its power, and managed it to the best of his ability. He ate a healthy diet, rarely indulging in dessert. He kept snacks handy—in the car, in his desk drawer, in his pocket—in case his blood sugar dropped. He kept insulin and syringes with him, in case his blood sugar spiked. As a young teenager, he had visited a doctor once a month to have his blood sugar checked; but as an adult, thanks to advances in medicine, he was able to check his own blood sugar—twice a day at first, and then, in his last ten years, multiple times every day. He took his medications religiously, checking them off on a long list morning and night. He stopped smoking when he realized smoking had contributed to the loss of one leg, and could take the other. He kept his doctor appointments and took advantage of every medical breakthrough he heard about.

"I understand they're doing pancreas transplants now," he said casually to his nephrologist at a routine appointment, seven years after receiving his first kidney. He had just read about that surgery in a magazine in the doctor's waiting room.

"Yes," the doctor said looking up from his paperwork. "They've made a lot of progress recently with the pancreas."

He paused, gazing straight at Tracy.

"Is that something you'd be interested in?"

Something you'd be interested in?

Tracy did not hesitate. The kidney was working well. A pancreas transplant would eliminate his insulin dependency. It might be new, it might still be in development, but of course he was interested. And so began that chapter in his life, and our life. Tracy enjoyed six years free of insulin injections, free to eat—or not eat—as he wished, all because he asked and was interested.

Not everyone was interested.

Many of Tracy's dialysis friends—in 1989 and again in 2002-04—were definitely not interested in a kidney transplant. Some were afraid of surgery. Some, no doubt, lacked the medical insurance to make it possible. Others figured, "I'm getting by. Why rock the boat?"

But Tracy was always interested. Any time there was a chance to push back at diabetes—through medicine, through technology, through surgery or lifestyle—Tracy took it. He made the most of his life, in every way that he could, for as long as he could.

The good news in 2014—ninety-three years after the discovery of insulin, fifty-three years after Tracy's diagnosis with Type I diabetes, twenty-five years after his first organ transplant—is that medical science has made remarkable advances in the treatment and understanding of diabetes. The tools and tests now available to help diabetics monitor and maintain proper blood sugar levels (including implanted insulin pumps and even blood-sugar sniffing service dogs), the surgical interventions including transplants that are now routine, the ever more sophisticated understanding of the interconnectedness of human systems: all of this makes diabetes potentially much more manageable.

In those same decades, the general public has become more aware of diabetes and much more willing to talk about it, just as we are more comfortable talking about other diseases that affect our communities and families. In Tracy's youth, afflictions of almost any kind were hush-hush subjects; no one discussed them openly. As a result, Tracy knew of only one other diabetic when he was in high school, another boy about his age who ultimately committed suicide. Today, both diabetes and organ transplants are regular topics in the news. Parents, children and teachers acknowledge the disease. Family members proudly donate healthy kidneys, sometimes even to strangers as part of an elaborate chain of interconnected transplants. Diabetic youngsters and teens routinely participate in the full range of kid activities including school sports. There are summer camps for diabetic kids, and plenty of diabetic cookbooks on bookstore shelves. Rocker Crystal Bowersox brought Type 1 diabetes to American Idol's national TV audience.

Clicking through cable TV channels with my remote recently, I encountered an upbeat show called "D-Life: Your Diabetes Life," which turned out to be all about living with the Type 1 disease. The episode I saw profiled boy-band heartthrob Nick Jonas, who lives with Type 1 diabetes, and documented the "Tour d'Afrique," a 120-day bicycling marathon across the African continent, where the cyclists managed their diabetes along with the demands of their extreme sport. The show also featured a prominent chef introducing several mouthwatering diabetic recipes, and a journalist interviewing seasoned diabetics about the experience of low blood sugar: "Does it still scare you when it happens?" the reporter asked.

"Every time," admitted a young man in his '30s, whose wry smile reminded me of Tracy.

A mass media program like this—highlighting the diverse accomplishments of diabetics in many fields, while highlighting the challenges of the disease and the treatments that can help diabetics follow their dreams—was unheard of until recently.

Like cancer (once referred to in a whisper as "the big C") and more recently HIV/AIDS, diabetes has come out into the open since Tracy was diagnosed. It is still a chronic disease and there is no cure, nor any definitive understanding of the causes, at least of Type 1. But no doctor today should need to tell an adolescent, newly diagnosed with Type 1 diabetes, "You don't need to worry about living past 40..."

That's the good news.

The bad news, however, is equally stunning.

Diabetes is still a potentially devastating disease, with consequences that still can include high blood pressure, kidney failure, nerve damage, blindness, amputations, heart disease, and—oh, yes—death.

Diabetes is expensive. Whether you respect it or ignore it, the disease has a huge impact on health care, health insurance, and every patient's household budget, with or without insurance. Recent news articles have tried to alert the public to the tremendous economic and medical impact that an increased incidence of the disease will have on our society.

Perhaps most disturbing of all, changes in society over the past few decades have contributed to an epidemic increase in Type 2 diabetes. Think about eating habits, for example. In the world I knew in 1960, food was something you ate at a table after someone (usually a woman, usually your mother) prepared it, combining ingredients and cooking for some period of time. Unless you were camping, or on a picnic, or maybe at the ball park, you came to the kitchen or the dining room for food, and you sat down to eat. Food was not something you ate in the car, or while you walked, or anytime you felt like it. Snacking was a cultural no-no at the time, and generally considered a sign of bad parenting. You ate your meals during meal times. On hot summer days, if you were lucky and your mom gave you the money, you might get an ice cream bar from the drive-by vendor with the sing-song jingle blaring from the truck—but that was about it for mobile eating. The "drive through" had not been invented and "fast food" was not yet in our vocabulary, let alone our neighborhood. Even processed food was not much of an option, limited mostly to hot dogs and Spam (with a capital S).

The same was true of beverages. Fifty years ago, no one drank coffee (with or without sugar, cream, syrup, cinnamon, peppermint or whipped cream) while walking or driving or dragging luggage through an airport, or doing anything other than sitting in a chair at a table or on a stool at a counter. No one arrived at someone else's house carrying a cappuccino or an open bottle of soda—especially if they were coming for dinner. No child expected to buy anything but milk in a school cafeteria.

Today, we eat and drink more things, in more places, at more times, with more freedom and to more excess than was imaginable in the past. And we do a lot of it from "to go" boxes and carry-out cups—"Tall, grande or jumbo?"

At the same time, even though we eat "on the go," we move around a lot less than we did in the past.

Few of us lead the active lives of our farmer ancestors. Almost no one walks to work. Fewer and fewer children walk to school. More kids and teenagers participate in organized sports—but hardly anyone just goes out to play. (Few families have a parent at home to send the kids outdoors after school or keep an eye on them through the window.) Cell phones, computers and remote controls have brought kids and adults indoors and put everyone onto the couch.

All of these conditions—a high-fat diet, 24/7 access to food, lack of exercise, and the resulting surge in obesity—have been identified as primary contributors to the explosion of what we once called adult-onset diabetes, when it was a disease of old people. (Only grandparents "got the sugar" back then.) When overweight children as young as 10 or 11 began showing up with the disease, the name changed. Today we call it Type 2 diabetes.

So there is the great irony. Progress—despite the knowledge, understanding and great good that it has brought about in so many ways—has also set in place the conditions that are making us an overweight and under-exercised society.

In other words, as medical science provides better and better treatment for diabetes, we seem bent on putting ourselves more and more at risk of it.

No one would argue that we should go back to the 1950s or '60s, even if we could; but reclaiming the increased physical activity and more disciplined eating habits of that era might go a long way toward slowing the development and incidence of Type 2 diabetes.

Recent research also has revealed unexplained increases in the prevalence of Type 1 diabetes. Medical science has yet to untangle the exact causes or triggers of what we once called "juvenile" diabetes; but diet and exercise are critical factors in managing and living with this form of the disease, just as they are for Type 2.

Tracy never wanted to be remembered as "a diabetic." I hope this account of our life together has not cast him in exactly the light he tried so hard to avoid. But I have always thought that he would be pleased to help encourage others to do what they can to avoid the ravages of this disease.

And now, as our youngest granddaughter adjusts to the diagnosis of Type 1 diabetes that came just two months after her eleventh birthday,

I believe Tracy would be passionate about encouraging her, and everyone else, to grab hold of this disease:

- to make exercise an integral part of an active daily life;
- to choose a healthy diet not dependent on fast food, salt, fat and sugary drinks;
- to take responsibility for personal health and follow doctors' orders so that small things do not become matters of life and death;
- and to take advantage of medical breakthroughs whenever possible.

He would tell our granddaughter to do all these things so that she, too, can live life to the fullest, nurturing her curiosity, pursuing her passions, and refusing to be defined by anything other than who she is in her heart and soul.

I believe he would want to say that. To her and to all of us.

I hope so.

References

Among the many books and dozens of articles over the past twenty-five years that have enhanced my understanding of the history and impact of diabetes, these stand out:

A Science Odyssey, 100 Years of Discovery, Charles Flowers
(William Morrow and Company, Inc., New York. 1998): biochemist J. B. Collip quoted on diabetes research, page 201.

The Journey of a Diabetic, Lawrence M. Pray
(Bookthrift Co., Revised Edition. 1987)

"The Conquest of Diabetes," J. M. Fenster
(American Heritage of Invention & Technology: Winter 1999)

"Bad Blood: Diabetes and Its Awful Toll Quietly Emerge as a Crisis," N. R. Kleinfield
(The New York Times: January 9, 2006)

Books about loss and grief alluded to in the text (especially in "Do This In Remembrance of Me") include:

The Year of Magical Thinking, Joan Didion
(Borzoi Book/Alfred A. Knopf, New York. 2005)

Here If You Need Me, Kate Braestrup
(Back Bay Books/Little, Brown & Company, New York. 2007)

The Eyes Are Sunlight, A Journey Through Grief, Shirley Koers
(Ave Maria Press, Notre Dame, IN. 1986)

References

The Shack, William Paul Young
(Windblown Media, Newbury Park, CA. 2007)

We Love You, Matty: Meeting Death with Faith, Tad Dunne
(Baywood Publishing Company, Inc., Amityville, NY. 2000)

Tear Soup: A Recipe for Healing After Loss, Pat Schwiebert and Chuck DeKlyen
(Grief Watch, Portland, Oregon. 1999)

Questions About Angels, Billy Collins
(University of Pittsburgh Press. 1991)

When Dinosaurs Die: A Guide to Understanding Death,
Laurie Krasny Brown and Marc Brown
(Little, Brown Books for Young Readers, 1998)

The following article was particularly helpful in considering end of life issues and medicine:

"Letting Go," Atul Gawande
(Annals of Medicine in The New Yorker: August 2, 2010)

The following hymns are quoted in the text:

"Breathe on Me, Breath of God" (Words: Edwin Hatch, 1835-1889, based on John 20:22; Music: Robert Jackson, 1842-1914)

"This Is My Father's World" (Words: Maltvie D. Babcock, 1858-1901; Music: Franklin L. Sheppard, 1852-1930)

"Lonesome Valley" (Traditional American gospel song)

"In the Garden" (Words and music: C. Austin Miles, 1912)